Developing a Local Curriculu

How can your local area become a source of inspiration for curriculum development? How can it enhance the teaching and learning at your school?

Developing a Local Curriculum explores how your local area and its resources can be used as a stimulus and inspiration for curriculum development. It examines the ways in which the geography, history, culture and people within your local area can enrich the learning experiences offered to students to make these experiences more relevant and meaningful.

Drawing on a wide range of examples from schools already taking this approach, the book shows how individual subjects can be developed through an understanding of the rich histories and cultures of the local area. It also reveals how engaging with the 'local' in education can help restore young people's sense of identity and community. The book's features include:

- practical guidance on engaging with the local community in innovative ways;
- suggestions for engagement with local cultural activities such as architecture, digital arts, theatre and film;
- ways to develop effective partnerships with local businesses and charities;
- detailed case studies showing how schools put the ideas described into practice.

This exciting new book aims to inspire you to develop a curriculum that is meaningful for pupils and gives them a strong sense of connection with their local area and understanding of its past, present and future.

William Evans is Senior Lecturer in Education at Manchester Metropolitan University, UK.

Jonathan Savage is Reader in Education and Enterprise Fellow at the Institute of Education, Manchester Metropolitan University, UK. He is also Managing Director of UCan Play, a not-for-profit company dedicated to supporting innovative approaches to education with technology.

Developing a Local Curriculum

Using your locality to inspire teaching and learning

William Evans and Jonathan Savage

Routledge
Taylor & Francis Group

LONDON AND NEW YORK

First published 2015
by Routledge
2 Park Square, Milton Park, Abingdon, Oxon OX14 4RN

and by Routledge
711 Third Avenue, New York, NY 10017

Routledge is an imprint of the Taylor and Francis Group, an informa business

© 2015 William Evans and Jonathan Savage

British Library Cataloguing in Publication Data
A catalogue record for this book is available from the British Library

Library of Congress Cataloging-in-Publication Data
Savage, Jonathan.
Developing a local curriculum : using your locality to inspire teaching and learning / Jonathan Savage and William Evans.
  pages cm
  1. Curriculum planning. 2. Education–Curricula. 3. Community and school.
  I. Evans, William (Senior lecturer) II. Title.
  LB2806.15.S29 2015
  375'.001–dc23   2014038778

ISBN: 978-0-415-70891-3 (hbk)
ISBN: 978-0-415-70892-0 (pbk)
ISBN: 978-1-315-71822-4 (ebk)

Typeset in Sabon
by Wearset Ltd, Boldon, Tyne and Wear

MIX
Paper from
responsible sources
FSC
www.fsc.org   FSC® C013056

Printed and bound in Great Britain by
TJ International Ltd, Padstow, Cornwall

Contents

Chapter 1

Area-based approaches to curriculum development

Why write a book on area-based approaches to curriculum development? For us, there are three main reasons. The first is personal; the second is political; and the third, and perhaps the most important, is pedagogical.

The personal dimension

The personal motivation for this book comes from our backgrounds as teachers and teacher educators. Will was bought up in Stoke on Trent and taught for a number of years in Wigan, in the north-west of England. Jonathan was bought up in Surrey, and taught during the 1990s in Suffolk, the most easterly county of England. Our stories and lives merged in Didsbury, in south Manchester, on one fateful day during the summer of 2001. We were both attending an interview for the same job – running the Postgraduate Certificate in Education (PGCE) in Music programme at what was then the Institute of Education, Manchester Metropolitan University.

Job interviews are always stressful. Along with a number of other candidates, we gave our presentations, had lunch and were interviewed. We cannot remember all the details, but we are sure there was a lot of macho posturing during the process. But at some point during the day we were informed that the university was not going to appoint one person, but two! That was a surprise to everyone. Following the completion of the day's activities, and while on our respective journeys home to Wigan and Suffolk, we both received phone calls that offered us our jobs. We have both done that job to the present day.

Working as a team over the last 13 years has been highly enjoyable. Anyone who knows us both will tell you that we are both very different from each other. Will is a northerner, Jonathan is a southerner; Will has a sharp sense of humour, Jonathan tries hard; Will rides his bike to work, Jonathan drives an old Mazda; Will has numerous sharp designs for facial hair; Jonathan is just glad he has some hair left. We could go on!

But there are also many things that we share. We had both worked in McDonalds at one point (Will was a manager, Jonathan got 'one star'), we both enjoy a round of golf, and we have both got impeccable dress sense.

Musically, although we have many differences (Jonathan was bought up playing classical percussion in an orchestra, Will was bought up in the brass band world playing the tuba), we have found common ground and understanding in our love for music and our commitment to developing the very best educational experiences for our pupils (in both the school and the university).

More seriously, though, the key things that make us both similar and different go back to some fundamental elements – our genes, our upbringing, our experiences in early life as shaped by our parents and our siblings, our schooling and, of course, where we were bought up and the communities within which we lived.

We have both become the people that we are today because of a complex web of people and places and their influences on our lives. The same is true for you and those you work with, including your teaching colleagues and your pupils. As we will be discussing throughout this book, teaching and curriculum development go hand-in-hand, and both need to be located within a local context in order to be truly effective. Who you are is shaped by where you have lived. Similarly, who you are as a teacher is shaped by where you teach. By this, we do not just mean the school where you are located. That school is situated in a locality, in an area, and that will influence the way that it educates its pupils. This book will explore how.

But before we explore further what we mean by an 'area-based' curriculum and how this might impact on your work, there is an important second dimension that we need to consider carefully: the political dimension.

The political dimension

Educational reform has always been very political! But perhaps this has been particularly obvious since 2010. During this time, the Department for Education, led by Michael Gove and his various colleagues, undertook a restructuring of the school system within the United Kingdom that has had significant consequences for the theme of this book. Although it is beyond the scope of our book to comment extensively on these reforms, we will say that it is our view that it is highly unlikely that these reforms will be overturned by a future government whatever their particular political 'colour'. For this reason, we have considered it important to outline how these political reforms have strengthened the need for this particular book.

One of the key elements of the educational reforms that have been implemented since 2010 is the strengthening of schools as independent, autonomous bodies with significant power to determine their own policies, practices and, importantly, curriculum. While the new National Curriculum, which covers all Key Stages, was implemented in September 2014, it is not really 'national' in any meaningful sense. Individual schools, such as academies and free schools are able to design and teach their own curricula. However, Ofsted (the Office for Standards in Education, Children's Services and Skills) will assess whether any individual school's 'alternative' curriculum is robust and fit for purpose.

This apparent 'loss' of the *national* curriculum has been bemoaned by some, while others have been quick to draw a distinction between curriculum frameworks which are external to the school, and the school curriculum itself which is central and internal to the school. In 2011, Tim Oates, the Chair of the Expert Panel for the National Curriculum Review, wrote:

> This distinction between the National Curriculum and the school curriculum is vital, and it's been lost. The National Curriculum is that which is stated in law. The school curriculum – what actually happens in a specific school with specific pupils – falls within the autonomy of the school and is critical in delivering

public and personal benefits, providing a safe environment where intensive learning can take place, and giving wide experience.

(Oates 2011, p. 30)

We are not so sure that schools make this subtle distinction. But there is no doubt that today schools are enjoying a considerable degree of freedom in this area compared to 10 years ago. This 'freedom' has extended to important pedagogical processes within the curriculum. An obvious example of this concerns assessment. Previous iterations of the National Curriculum contained attainment targets and assessment levels. From this baseline, schools invented all kinds of data-driven approaches to monitoring pupils' development including approaches to baselining, benchmarking and target setting. This had a profound effect on how you, as a teacher, had to justify the progress that your pupils have made in your subject or year, as well as how you communicated that progress to senior managers and parents. Much of this is now changing.

This government has viewed many of these practices as unhelpful. By removing these assessment elements from the National Curriculum they are handing over responsibility for when and how pupils are assessed to individual schools. Their expectation is that schools will embrace this freedom and find new ways to assess their pupils that are relevant and appropriate within their local context (and these approaches will be evaluated and judged through the inspection process). Time will tell whether or not these reforms initiate and sustain a more productive model of assessment in our schools. But the key point is clear – schools are now more autonomous than ever. There is a greater degree of opportunity and flexibility for schools to operate very differently from each other. Part of this shift could involve schools working much more closely with their local communities and reflecting key attributes of that in their curriculum arrangements: an area-based curriculum.

But there is an important flip side to this coin that directly impacts on the broader considerations of this book. In terms of school governance, many of the reforms initiated since 2010 have resulted in schools being distanced from their local communities. Links with local authorities are being dismantled, private companies with 'chains' (what an unfortunate word) of schools are being favoured, and many schools are being forced to become independent academies. Why is this such a big deal? Well, in the process of becoming an academy all of the school's assets including its grounds, its buildings and staff are taken out of local authority control and placed under the control of that academy's trustees. Trustees are not school governors (although individual governors may become trustees). The processes by which trustees are nominated and appointed are highly variable. Local representation at the level of these trustees is also highly variable and there is no requirement for trustees to be members of the local community that the school serves. Local communities are losing direct influence over and control of their schools and this is highly contentious (but also, sadly, largely unnoticed by local communities).

These significant changes in educational policy have been highlighted and discussed in a range of educational debates spanning back many years (Elliot 1998; Barber 2001). More recently, Hargreaves (2009) anticipated that we would move towards a decentralisation of educational policy that would result in a 'post-standardisation' era in education through which curriculum design would inevitably become devolved to local regions and the schools therein. This is precisely what is happening today.

Previous versions of the National Curriculum (especially the one implemented in 2007) explicitly acknowledged this and built on this principle as one of its core values. It promoted 'greater flexibility and coherence' among its core messages, expressing a key aim as empowering schools to 'personalise learning experiences and meet their learners' through 'less prescribed subject content'. In particular, the National Curriculum, it was hoped, would allow each school to 'design and build its own locally determined curriculum that matches the ethos of the school, the needs and capabilities of its community of learners and the local context' (QCA 2007, p. 5).

We would echo the importance of these aspirations. While the current National Curriculum is very short on rhetoric such as this, rightly or wrongly, it does give this freedom directly to schools in alternative ways.

However, this is not a golden bullet. It is important to remember that in the United Kingdom's recent history alternative approaches to curriculum development have been facilitated and rejected. Prior to the first National Curriculum (implemented in 1992), there was a long period of progressive educational practice that was rooted in school-based curriculum development. There was a huge variety and diversity of practice, including active experiential learning approaches, negotiated tasks, project-based and thematically based programmes, blurred curriculum and subject boundaries, and much more besides (MacDonald and Walker 1976). The unevenness and patchiness of such approaches was one of the significant reasons why the National Curriculum was introduced, as was their incapacity to challenge in any substantial or meaningful way the issue of educational disadvantage (Thomson and Hall 2008).

For us, there is one important element in this discussion that is largely missing so far. That missing element is you, the teacher! Whatever the policy frameworks that are in play within a particular political age, your work with your pupils should be central to your thinking about curriculum development. It is to this dimension that we turn our attention now, through a quote from the writing of Elliot Eisner:

> Those interested in curriculum matters and working with teachers ... recognise that the conditions teachers addressed were each distinctive. As a result, abstract theory would be of limited value. Each child needed to be known individually ... each situation ... was unique. It was a grasp of these distinctive features that teachers needed ... to make good decisions in the classroom.
>
> (Eisner 2002, p. 381)

The pedagogical dimension

In Facer's phrase, 'teachers are the curriculum makers' (Facer 2014, p. 3). It is through your understanding of your school and your pupils, through your assumptions and your beliefs about teaching and learning, that the creation and enactment of a curriculum is facilitated.

Curriculum development of this type is a core element of every teacher's work. We would argue that the process of constructing and delivering a curriculum is far more than a simple reorganisation of bodies of knowledge within a subject area.

Built around processes of reflective inquiry, action research and collaborative mechanisms that help you and your colleagues work together, curriculum development can become an important site of professional development that can be beneficial for yourself and your school.

More than half a century ago, the Crowther Report stated that 'everything in education depends ultimately on the teacher' (Central Advisory Council for Education 1959). It is a sentiment that one of the greatest educational thinkers of recent decades, Lawrence Stenhouse, would have undoubtedly agreed with. Stenhouse was a firm advocate for the teacher. It was fitting that the teachers with whom he worked across East Anglia contributed a plaque in his memory. On it, they inscribed Stenhouse's own words: 'It is the teachers who in the end will change the world of the school by understanding it' (Stenhouse 1975, p. 208).

Stenhouse was well known for his belief that teachers could enhance their professional understanding by engaging in processes of curriculum development and educational research. His notion of the 'teacher as researcher' has done much to shape current thinking about professional development, reflective practice and action research. He was an outspoken critic of what he saw as the de-professionalisation of the teacher through 'objectives-based' curriculum models such as the National Curriculum or those set out within national framework for numeracy or literacy. This approach, he said,

> rests on an acceptance of the teacher as a kind of intellectual navvy. An objectives-based curriculum is like a site plan simplified so that people know exactly where to dig their trenches without having to know why.
>
> (Stenhouse 1980, p. 85)

For Stenhouse, such curriculum models were a symbol of distrust of the teacher. He worked hard to challenge such approaches. More than that, he developed alternative ideas that reasserted the teachers' role in curriculum planning and development. If, as he wrote, 'it seems odd to minimise the use of the most expensive resource in the school' (Stenhouse 1975, p. 24), it would be better to 'reinvest in the teacher and to construct the curriculum in ways that would enhance teachers' understanding and capability' (Stenhouse 1980, p. 5).

These are powerful arguments that have much resonance with current thinking about curriculum design and development. As we will go on to see, recent pieces of curriculum reform have placed a greater degree of ownership and responsibility on schools. Every school's greatest asset is its teaching staff. The 'localisation' of the National Curriculum presents an opportunity for teachers to respond to the challenge of developing themselves and the curriculum they offer to their pupils in tandem. Developing an understanding of what is meant by an 'area-based curriculum' and using this knowledge to help develop your own curriculum planning is the central objective of this book.

Defining an area-based curriculum

These three dimensions – the personal, the political and the pedagogical – are important starting points for our book. As we have sought to understand our personal motivations, the political climate and the centrality of pedagogy to curriculum development, we have come to an understanding together about the potential importance of an area-based curriculum approach for our schools. But what precisely do we mean by an 'area-based curriculum'?

We are happy to align our thinking here with the RSA (Royal Society for the encouragement of Arts, Manufactures and Commerce), and define an 'area-based curriculum' as:

> An enhancement of the educational experiences of young people by creating rich connections with the communities, cities and cultures that surround them and by distributing the education effort across the people, organisations and institutions of a local area.
>
> (RSA 2009)

This definition has two main components. First, it is about schools and teachers making connections with their local communities, villages, towns or cities and the various elements of their locality; second, it is about seeing education as something done in partnership with other people, organisations and institutions throughout the local area. In other words, it is about sharing the responsibility for the education of our young people with a greater number of partners. This second strand is vitally important and will be picked up in further detail in the final two chapters of our book. But please note this now. Sharing the responsibility to educate our young people with others does not mean that schools should neglect their own responsibilities. Partnership working is good, but schools have a set of experience, competences and skills that other partners may not have; schools have to be able to assure the quality of the process and practice of an area-based curriculum approach when other partners are involved.

As the RSA have developed their work in this field, various alternative definitions and statements of what constitutes as an area-based curriculum have evolved. Their recent work describes an area-based curriculum as one that is:

- *About* a place: making use of local context and resources to frame learning;
- *By* a place: designed by schools in partnership with other local stakeholders; and
- *For* a place: meeting the specific needs of children and local communities.

> (RSA 2012, p. 5)

This summarises, very well in our opinion, the approach that we are going to adopt within this book. The RSA go on to provide a set of objectives for an area-based curriculum, namely that it should:

- Create learning experiences that are engaging for children from all backgrounds;
- Increase children's understanding of and attachment to the place where they live;
- Embed schools more deeply within their communities and localities.

> (Ibid.)

Prioritising planning

How can an area-based curriculum approach be developed? There are various ways, and we will be drawing on a range of examples throughout this book. But, right at the outset, we want to emphasise that there is a massive amount that you, as an individual teacher, can achieve. The most important element in this mix is you!

Effective planning is central to an effective pedagogy. Elsewhere (Savage 2014) we have written about what such planning entails and how it can be done well. We will not be repeating all that key content here. For now, we want to identify the three main locations of planning where your area-based curriculum could be developed. We also want to use this opportunity to define a few key terms that will become important throughout the following chapters.

For us, curriculum development covers three major strands of planning: long-, medium- and short-term planning.

Long-term planning

For longer-term planning, the temptation can be to rely too heavily on external frameworks such as the Early Years Foundation Framework, the National Curriculum or GCSE specifications for a particular subject. While these frameworks do have value, they are not what we mean by longer-term planning. You should not rely on these solely as your long-term plan. Longer-term planning involves thinking about the units of work that compromise a whole Key Stage's work. By its nature, it is concerned with an overview of curriculum content, key teaching strategies and learning opportunities that will be developed through the medium-term planning. There is no doubt that a longer-term plan will reflect the key concepts and processes contained within the appropriate National Curriculum documentation, or the main learning objectives or targets of a GCSE specification, but these, on their own, will not constitute an effective longer-term curriculum plan.

Medium-term planning

In medium-term planning, the process of curriculum development becomes a little more detailed and precise. Medium-term plans can be thought of as 'units of work'. Each unit of work will have a set of key learning objectives and learning outcomes; will identify key resources and strategies for assessment, personalisation and differentiation; and will outline a broad description of the teaching activities and the learning therein. Units of work may last a number of weeks, or a whole term. There is no magic formula for their length! However, they are building-blocks of the curriculum development process that link the longer-term planning to the short-term planning, i.e. the individual lesson plans.

Short-term or lesson planning

Lesson plans contain all the information that you need prepare for, teach and evaluate an individual lesson. Lesson planning itself is a highly skilled activity (and you can read more about how to do this well in Savage 2014). Done well, it will challenge the way you think and act within the classroom and should be conceptualised as an integral part of your pedagogy, your 'way of being' as a teacher. Lesson planning is too important to be left to chance. In the early stages of your teaching career it is likely that most of your time will be spent thinking about curriculum development at this level.

This book explores how your local area can become a foundational and integral part of your curriculum development. This could take place at any of the above three levels (long-, medium- or short-term planning).

It seems clear to us that unless the key aims and objectives of an area-based curriculum are considered in each of these three key locations then your approach to facilitate an area-based curriculum will probably fail.

In the following chapters we will be considering all of these locations in further details. We will give examples of projects drawn from our own and others' work that illustrate these key concepts. We will be asking you to engage in a number of simple tasks, both practical and reflective, to facilitate your work in this area.

References

Barber, M. (2001) 'High Expectations and Standards for All, No Matter What: Creating a world class education service in England'. In Fielding, M. (ed.) *Taking Education Really Seriously: Four Years' Hard Labour*. London, Routledge.

Central Advisory Council for Education (1959) *The Crowther Report, 15 to 18 Vol. 1*. London, HMSO.

Eisner, E. (2002) 'From Episteme to Phreonesis to Artistry in the Study and Improvement of Teaching'. *Teaching and Teacher Education* 18:4, pp. 375–385.

Elliot, J. (1998) *The Curriculum Experiment: Meeting the Challenge of Social Change*. Buckingham, Open University Press.

Facer, K. (2014) 'Towards an Area-based Curriculum: Insights and directions from the research'. www.thersa.org/__data/assets/pdf_file/0009/286983/116821106-Manchester-Curriculum-Report-FINAL.pdf [last accessed 14 February 2014].

Hargreaves, A. (2009) 'The Coming of Post-standardisation: Three weddings and a funeral'. In Sugrue, C. (ed.) *The Future of Educational Change: International Perspectives*. London, Routledge.

MacDonald, B. and Walker, R. (1976) *Changing the Curriculum*. London, Open Books.

Oates, T. (2011) 'Why England is Flagging'. *Leadership Focus* May/June, pp. 30–32.

QCA (Qualifications and Curriculum Authority) (2007) *The New Secondary Curriculum: What has changed and why?* London, QCA.

RSA (Royal Society for the encouragement of Arts, Manufactures and Commerce) (2009) *Towards an Area-based Curriculum: Insights and directions from the research*. London, RSA.

RSA (2012) *Thinking about an Area-based Curriculum: A guide for practitioners*. London, RSA.

Savage, J. (2014) *Lesson Planning: Key concepts and skills for teachers*. London, Routledge.

Stenhouse, L. (1975) *An Introduction to Curriculum Research and Development*. London, Heinemann Educational.

Stenhouse, L. (1980) 'Product or Process? A reply to Brian Crittenden'. Reprinted in Ruddock, J. and Hopkins, D. (eds) (1985) *Research as a Basis for Teaching*. London, Heinemann Educational.

Thomson, P. and Hall, C. (2008) 'Opportunities Missed and/or Thwarted? Funds of knowledge meet the English national curriculum'. *Curriculum Journal* 19:2, pp. 87–103.

Chapter 2

The geography of place

Introduction

In the next four chapters we will be exploring how different features or characteristics of your locality can be used as a stimulus for an area-based curriculum development approach. The four characteristics that we are going to use are the geography (this chapter), history (Chapter 3), culture (Chapter 4) and community (Chapter 5) of a local area. In doing so, we realise that these divisions are a little arbitrary. However, they will give us a series of simple starting points from which we can explore our book's key themes. As with all simple categorisations, please do not allow the terms themselves that we are using to limit your imagination. There will be numerous points of overlap within these four chapters, and the opportunities to forge creative links between categories and approaches will be encouraged throughout.

This chapter will explore approaches to an area-based curriculum development approach that utilises the geographical features of a local area as a stimulus. The principal way in which we will consider this is through an analysis of five case studies drawn from work conducted by different teachers in varying locations across the country. In focusing on the 'geography' of a place, we are not suggesting that you will need to become a teacher of geography! Rather, this chapter will explore how the geography of a place can inspire and facilitate your construction of a curriculum in whatever subject or phase of education you work within.

In the previous chapter, we introduced a definition for an area-based curriculum developed by the RSA. They describe an area-based curriculum as one that is:

- *About* a place: making use of local context and resources to frame learning;
- *By* a place: designed by schools in partnership with other local stakeholders; and
- *For* a place: meeting the specific needs of children and local communities.

(RSA 2012, p. 5)

The objectives of such a curriculum were to:

- Create learning experiences that are engaging for children from all backgrounds;
- Increase children's understanding of and attachment to the place where they live;
- Embed schools more deeply within their communities and localities.

(Ibid.)

In this chapter, we will be drawing explicitly on the first part of the RSA definition (i.e. the locally-based curriculum being *about* a place) and on the second of their key objectives – increasing pupils' understanding of and attachment to the physical place in which they live. In doing so, we are not negating the importance of a holistic understanding of the RSA definition and objectives. Rather, we are positioning these chapters in a slightly more focused way in order to develop our own arguments as to what constitutes an area-based curriculum development approach.

The academic discipline of geography contains a number of different approaches. The word 'geography' comes from the Greek meaning 'earth description'; a literal definition would be 'to write about or describe the earth'. Various branches of geography have emerged over the years, the two principal ones being physical geography (the study of the earth itself) and human geography (the study of the patterns and processes that shape how humans engage with their environment; this could include political, cultural, social and economic dimensions).

Understanding geography

Although this chapter is not about teaching geography, it is important to gain an overview of the broad types of knowledge and understanding that your pupils will have in relation to geography as an academic subject, in order to inform your own understanding of how the geographical features of your local area could helpfully inform the construction of an area-based curriculum approach in your own teaching.

To this end, the National Curriculum contains the following statement about why it is important that all pupils should develop their knowledge, skills and understanding in geography:

> A high-quality geography education should inspire in pupils a curiosity and fascination about the world and its people that will remain with them for the rest of their lives. Teaching should equip pupils with knowledge about diverse places, people, resources and natural and human environments, together with a deep understanding of the Earth's key physical and human processes. As pupils progress, their growing knowledge about the world should help them to deepen their understanding of the interaction between physical and human processes, and of the formation and use of landscapes and environments. Geographical knowledge, understanding and skills provide the framework and approaches that explain how the Earth's features at different scales are shaped, interconnected and change over time.
>
> (DfE 2014)

Specific aims of the National Curriculum for Geography are described as enabling pupils to:

- Develop contextual knowledge of the location of globally significant places – both terrestrial and marine – including their defining physical and human characteristics and how these provide a geographical context for understanding the actions of processes;

- Understand the processes that give rise to key physical and human geographical features of the world, how these are interdependent and how they bring about spatial variation and change over time.

(Ibid.)

The skills that pupils will be acquiring through their study of geography will include being able to:

- Collect, analyse and communicate with a range of data gathered through experiences of fieldwork that deepen their understanding of geographical processes;
- Interpret a range of sources of geographical information, including maps, diagrams, globes, aerial photographs and Geographical Information Systems (GIS);
- Communicate geographical information in a variety of ways, including through maps, numerical and quantitative skills and writing at length.

(Ibid.)

Drawing on these themes relating to knowledge, skills and understanding that pupils will develop through learning about geography throughout their education, it is possible to begin to establish a broad range of potential approaches that could be adopted by which the geography of a particular place could begin to inform an approach to curriculum development. But before we do that, have a go at the following reflective task.

Reflective task

Consider the following two questions:

- What key principles or processes can you take from the statements above, relating to the key understanding, aims and skills associated with the academic subject of geography, that could be applied to a process of area-based curriculum development?
- To what extent are the principles and processes presented in the above statement suitable as a focal point for planning a new piece of area-based curriculum development?

Case studies

Our opening case study is a simple one. It describes one lesson observed within a unit of work being delivered to a group of Year 7 pupils. As you read it, consider to what extent the teacher's stated aim of helping their pupils learn about their locality was achieved.

Case Study 1 Designing and evaluating a locality-based monopoly-style board game

This was the last of a series of 12 one-hour lessons. The teacher wanted the Year 7 pupils to develop their skills of teamwork, negotiation, communication, cooperation and delegation. She also wanted the pupils to develop their understanding of the locality in which they lived. At the beginning of the lesson the teacher praised the pupils' efforts over the last half term. They had, in groups of four, all produced their own local monopoly-style games – one game per group.

All of the colourful boards were handed out. The teacher recapped the skills the class had developed over the last six weeks by asking closed questions. Individuals answered with words such as 'teamwork' and 'negotiation'. The teacher also stressed to the class that they had learnt about the geography of their local area. The rest of the lesson was simple. In groups of four the pupils were going to play their games. After that, they were going to evaluate them.

The pupils were well behaved and enjoyed the fruits of their labour. In discussions with each group, it became clear that they had had to work together to create and develop their games. Some groups did this very well and democratically. Inevitably, some did not and individuals felt that some members had not pulled their weight.

When asked questions about the subject-specific knowledge and skills that had been developed about the locality, the pupils' answers were vaguer. They had not been out to visit the local area to research their games. They had not considered the pricing of houses or streets when they decided where to put the streets on the board. When they were designing the 'Community Chest' or 'Chance' cards, the teacher had not encouraged them to make cards which would give the players new knowledge of the locality in which they lived or the rich history of the local area. One card read, 'Your dog bit someone – pay a fine of 10 pounds'!

The pupils clearly enjoyed playing the games. After they had finished it was time for the class to review and evaluate them. The teacher asked the class to decide on the criteria that could be used to judge whether the games were good. She wrote the agreed criteria on the board. They included points such as 'fun to play' and 'colourfully designed'. However, the teacher did not encourage the class to think about criteria linked to geographical or historical skills or knowledge. This was surprising as the scheme of work was designed around a theme that related learning to a local context (Harris *et al.* 2012, pp. 48–49).

There is no doubt that this lesson had some positive elements within it. These included:

- A range of well-developed teaching skills, including the design of an engaging game, effective behavior management, good questioning and answering skills, and modelling;
- The identification of a set of learning competencies that were facilitated and engaged with by pupils in a basic way;
- Some effective student-led evaluation activities.

However, in other ways the key learning within this lesson was under-theorised and under-developed. The construction of a monopoly-themed game was an ideal opportunity for pupils to use the content of the locality to develop their understanding of space and place and, from this, to extend it beyond the geography of the locality into other curriculum areas too (e.g. history and citizenship). Key resources such as maps, photographs, aerial photographs or other materials that document the locality could have been brought into the classroom to assist the generation of pupils' understanding at a deeper level. Key questions such as 'What is this place like?' and 'Why is it like this?' could have been considered. Broader questions such as 'How has this placed changed?' or 'How is it changing?' could have incorporated aspects of the recent history of the locality into the lesson most productively. Similar issues related to the identity and diversity of the people living within the local area could have also been considered.

The vast majority of these opportunities were not enacted within the lesson in any meaningful way. In this instance, the teacher's conceptual grasp of the humanities (especially geography and history) were weak and a generic set of learning competencies were superimposed on to the unit to such an extent that meaningful, area-based learning of the type we are promoting in this chapter was minimal.

This opening case study contrasts strongly with Case Study 2 below. But before you read it, please consider the questions below in the practical task.

Practical task

Case Study 2 is a review of a different lesson that explored a particular locality with a group of Year 7 pupils. It was taught by a history specialist who had worked very closely with a geography colleague to plan and resource the unit of work. The unit of work was designed to help the pupils develop their understanding of the locality within which they lived. Ask yourself the following questions:

- What concepts from your understanding of the geography (as an academic subject described in the opening of this chapter) would you expect to see developed in this lesson?
- What points from your own criteria for effective teaching (regardless of your own subject specialism) would you hope to see in the lesson?
- As you read Case Study 2, does the teacher develop the concepts that you predicted? What elements of effective teaching can you spot? What advice would you give the teacher to help him develop his teaching even further?
- And, most importantly for our chapter, how is the locality within which the pupils live used as a stimulus to help them learn effectively in this lesson?

Case Study 2 The shabbiest street in Britain

This was the first session of a two-week enrichment programme. The lesson started with the teacher showing the class a series of photographs. Could they work out what they were and where they were? After the second image it became clear to the children that the photographs were all taken in their local area.

They all easily identified the local leisure centre, the theatre and the library. All hands shot up when the next image was projected. The teacher then asked them if they could locate the images on a map of the local area. He was checking to see how much they understood about their locality and their sense of place. Clearly the pupils knew their stuff as they confidently pinpointed the locations of all five photographs. Next, the teacher introduced an aerial photograph of another location in the local area. Could the class work out where it was? The photograph depicted a concrete car park and street located next to Worthing train station. The car park was situated on the site of a 1960s-style shopping precinct that 30 years before had been the height of modern architecture. By the mid-1990s it had begun to appear dilapidated and was then demolished. Nothing

replaced it. The class immediately recognised the place as Teville Gate, and again confidently located the car park and street on the map.

The teacher then handed out a newspaper report. The headline read: 'Is this the
shabbiest street in Britain?' The class read through the first two paragraphs and realised
that the report was describing their local car park and street. At this point the teacher
introduced the enquiry question – 'Has Teville Gate always been the shabbiest street in
Britain?' The challenge had been set. But how would the class go about finding out?
The teacher asked what evidence they would need to work out the answer. Pairs discussed this for a couple of minutes and then fed back ideas such as asking people,
looking at maps, reading newspaper reports and going to the library to find local
history books.

The teacher then started to distribute a series of maps of the Teville Gate area. Pupils
worked in pairs and threes. The first was from 2010. After the class gained their bear-
ings with the maps – they located the train station, the car park and Teville Road – the
teacher introduced a second map, this time from 1970. They were asked to identify anything that had changed between 1970 and 2010. Little had changed; they could see that
the train station and the car park were still there, but the precinct that had recently been
knocked down had been standing in 1970. A further map was then distributed, this
time from 1952. At this point the class noticed a number of important changes. The car
park and the shopping precinct had vanished. Instead it seemed that houses with
gardens stood where the car park now was and the precinct had been. This was a dramatic change.

The teacher asked if we could tell what the houses were like from the map. Some of
theme were clearly bigger than the others and had longer gardens; some were connected
together in a terrace. The teacher then introduced a map from 1910 which still displayed the same houses, but this time a stream appeared at the end of some of the
gardens. A map from 1870 again clearly showed the same houses. A final map from
1848 was introduced. This time there were no houses, just fields. The only similarity to
today was the existence of the train station.

At this point the class were encouraged to come up with their own questions. What
were the houses from the nineteenth century actually like? Why had they been knocked
down? Who lived in them? What were these people like? The teacher wrote the questions on the board and explained that if they could find out the answer to these questions they could work out the answers to the big enquiry question: had Teville Gate
always been the shabbiest street in Britain? Clearly the map showed that the area had
changed over time, and the children had realised that the two biggest changes had happened between 1840 and 1870 and then between 1952 and 1970. But they needed more
evidence to really get a sense of place and understand change in a deeper sense.

At this point the teacher introduced a photograph of the street dating from 1900.
There was a horse and cart and a row of chimneys, but the style and size of the houses
were obscured by an avenue of trees. Although the houses looked as if they might be
large, using the photograph one simply couldn't tell exactly what they were like. The
class were asked how else they could find out. The teacher listened attentively to
answers before introducing some new evidence – a part of the 1891 census for the
Teville Gate area. Each pupil was given a character who appeared in the census and
lived in a house in the street. They were given the person's name and address,
and their age, their marital status and their job. The class were asked to walk around
and mix with each other to find the other people who lived with them in the same
house. They really enjoyed doing this. After about five minutes they had found their
families, lodgers and servants. They were then told that they were at a street party
and that they should meet their neighbours. They went around introducing themselves
to each other.

The teacher then asked them to create a continuum of social standing – with the most important person at one end and the least important at the other. The class did this well. Each person in the line described who they were and why they were standing where they were. Through this process it became clear that the people who lived in the street were quite wealthy, some had servants, and others had retired and lived off 'their own means'. The teacher then reminded the class of the enquiry question: Had Teville Gate always been the shabbiest street in Britain? The pupils now had enough evidence to make a more informed judgement. They said that it hadn't been that shabby in 1890 because the census suggested otherwise and this agreed with what they thought the photographs had shown. Their inference was that some of the houses were large – because, using the census material, the people who lived in them appeared to be wealthy.

The scheme of work then allowed the children to go for a walk and visit the Teville Gate area; it also helped the class understand how and why the houses had been knocked down, and they came up with their own regeneration scheme for the are which they designed and presented to local businessmen and members of the council (Harris *et al.* 2012, pp. 50–52).

This case study presents a fascinating and illuminating account of how one teacher used a certain part of his school's locality as a stimulus for an area-based curriculum. Although the majority of the learning here was situated within the subject areas of geography and history, there are key references and processes from other curriculum areas too, including drama, English, design and technology, and citizenship. It is an excellent example of cross-curricularity and an area-based curriculum approach.

There are a number of key strengths here that we would like to dwell on briefly. First, the lesson utilised subject content from a range of subject areas but it did so in a way that did not diminish those subject areas in any way. It respected the content and ways of working inherent within those subjects but brought them together within a common location – Teville Gate.

Second, the unit of work was written by a teacher who had a very strong grasp of his own subject area, but was willing to work collaboratively with others (in this case a geography colleague) in order to broaden the consideration of the locality in a meaningful and constructive way for his pupils. This complementary approach to in subject knowledge and subject pedagogy is very strong within this case study.

Third, the learning objectives underpinning this lesson were very strong. They related clearly and precisely to the development of pupils' knowledge of the locality within which they lived. The application of this local knowledge, in terms of the geographical and historical features, would be crucial in terms of pupils being able to reimagine their locality within their proposed regeneration schemes.

In terms of the conceptual planning that underpinned this unit, both teachers had established a very clear set of concepts that informed the design of the curriculum. The geographical concepts related to space and place; the historical concepts were change, continuity and causation. The interrelationship between these sets of concepts provided a very strong narrative for the unit that ensured that the key learning objectives were met in a powerful way.

In addition to the strong conceptual framework, the learning outcomes were clearly established, the resources were well prepared and the activities were engaging.

Key learning competencies (e.g. working in a group) were evident but were not allowed to dominate the curriculum planning (and certainly not to the extent that we considered in Case Study 1).

Finally, in addition to the learning objectives and the conceptual elements of the curriculum development, the pedagogical processes by which the teacher taught and pupils learnt were clearly identified. An enquiry-based approach has a long and established tradition in the humanities. It is beyond the scope of this book to examine this in detail. A general point will suffice. Adopting a cross-curricular approach to an area-based curriculum does not mean that well-established subject pedagogical approaches need to be sacrificed. Rather, they should be utilised and built up in imaginative ways (as in this case study).

The next case study is drawn from the work of one of the authors with a colleague (Savage and Challis 2001) at a high school in rural Suffolk. It has been chosen for inclusion within this chapter because it demonstrates effectively many of the key principles made above about how to explore your local area as a theme for curriculum development.

The case study was a pivotal moment for the author concerned. It was initiated and sustained through a close working professional relationship with one of the mathematics teachers (Mike Challis) at the school who, coincidentally, was also studying for a PhD at the same university department as the author. This case study was written shortly after the events unfolded and has been edited slightly for this publication.

Case Study 3 The *Dunwich Revisited* project

> A new world is coming
> And we don't know
> Just where we're going next.
> The old world is gone
> And never to be found.
> The past is in the past.
> So say your prayers and say goodbye,
> Say goodbye.
>   (Song composed by a group of Year
>   8 girls within their music lesson as
>   part of *Dunwich Revisited*)

This case study shares ideas, images, thoughts and judgements about a curriculum project, *Dunwich Revisited*, which took place at Debenham High School during January to March 2000. Through a description of the project and a sharing of the case study data, the events that took place within the classroom sessions, during the extra-curricular rehearsals and, finally, on the concert hall stage will be discussed.

Situated on the east coast of Suffolk, the former city of Dunwich has had a rich and interesting history. During the early part of the second millennium, it became a major port enjoying considerable wealth and prosperity. But due to the changing coastline, the emergence of a new river mouth further up the coast, and the silting up of its own port, Dunwich lost its place as the premier port on the east coast. Its source of prosperity was removed and the city itself eroded. During the next few hundred years most of the city was subsumed by the sea. Early last century All Saints Church, at one time the largest church in Dunwich, gradually fell from the top of the cliffs into the sea. Photographs of this event taken over a period of time provided a major stimulus to the project. Visitors to Dunwich today will find a beautiful beach, sandy cliffs and the odd fishing shack.

The story of Dunwich has become a rich source of inspiration for poets, artists and composers. In 1989, Mike Challis, a local composer and teacher of mathematics at the high school, was asked to compose a piece of music to accompany a dance, 'States of Sea', to be performed by Splinters Youth Dance Group at Snape Maltings Concert Hall. This piece, called *Dunwich*, represented the changing landscape of Dunwich through its ternary (arch) shape. The opening section depicted the natural environment of the landscape that became Dunwich. The second section described the conquering of the natural forces of the environment and subsequent human inhabitation (through two medieval-like dance melodies). The final section portrayed the powerful natural elements reclaiming and overcoming these human interactions (in a return to the opening music).

In documentation made available to pupils during the *Dunwich Revisited* project, the choreographer of 'States of the Sea', Pamela Harling-Challis, Mike Challis's wife, wrote about the initial inspiration for her dance and the accompanying music:

> I grew up in a desert, a kind of sea filled with waves of sand, howling wind, masses of sky and immense distance. 'States of the Sea' is about a desert, where water comes between sand and sky. It is about time, change and the relentless pressure of the elements.
>
> The desert, the sea, the imagery of the Beaufort Scale, Dunwich Heath and the photographic remains of All Saints Church are all sources of inspiration.

Many of these geographical features of local area became inspirations for the pupils as they began to think about how they could reinterpret the story of Dunwich for themselves.

Mike Challis's composition *Dunwich* became the focus for a composition project involving the whole of Years 7, 8 and 9, about 230 pupils in total, and the GCSE music group in Year 10 (15 pupils). Pupils were introduced to the place of Dunwich and its history before listening to the original piece. They were asked to make a series of responses to Challis's music, considering the mood, atmosphere and emotion of its various sections. The responses from each class formed part of a large wall display that later became a focus for an exchange of ideas and starting points for composition work. Pupils were then asked to spend time considering what type of sounds they might want to include in their own musical interpretation of Dunwich's history. They were encouraged to think of sounds that could be produced through using conventional instruments, voices, various technologies, or by selecting samples of environmental sounds that could be digitally imported into their pieces.

Subsequent lessons involved pupils choosing ideas from these sheets and composing short sound ideas. Pupils made these ideas using a variety of technologies. The primary method was the use of a microphone connected to a simple sound processor/monitor set-up. Pupils experimented with various instrumental or vocal sound sources, applying different types of effect to create the desired mood and atmosphere.

In addition to this way of working, other pupils in the GCSE class recorded environmental sounds on a portable minidisc player. These sounds were then imported into a computer running a digital audio mixing program (ProTools) before being edited using different pieces of computer software such as SoundHack, SoundEffects and Metasynth. All of these sound ideas were collected on the minidisc player and carefully labelled in preparation for the next stage of the project. These sound ideas would eventually form the sonic material for pupils' own Dunwich pieces.

As well as the individual class pieces that the pupils produced, an open session was held during lunchtime to select sound ideas for a whole school performance piece. This piece would be played at Snape Maltings Concert Hall as part of the annual Suffolk Celebration of Schools' Music. This annual event is intended to provide a platform for pupils' performance and composition work. It is a non-competitive music festival with entries from primary and high schools around Suffolk.

All pupils involved in the project were invited to come and 'audition' each of the short sound ideas. Using a series of simple star ratings, the 45 pupils who volunteered voted on which sounds they considered the most imaginative and appropriate for inclusion in this final piece. Out of 108 short sound ideas, 24 received five or more three-star votes. These sounds were to become the principal sonic material for the live performance piece. A group of 35 pupils, some volunteers and some selected, began rehearsals as an extracurricular activity in preparation for the performance.

After the democratic selection of the various sound ideas to be included in the piece, lunchtime rehearsals enabled the various sections to be assembled. Work on the instrumental and vocal parts was carried out at the same time as the assembly of computer-generated sounds and the DJ elements of the piece. The ternary structure of the original *Dunwich* piece was used, with particular attention being paid to the transition points between sections. The 'merging' together of the various ideas involved considerable discussion between pupils, Mike Challis and Jonathan Savage. The teachers were both keen to ensure that pupils had the final say as to what particular sound idea would go where in the final 'mix'. When there were disagreements between pupils, the teachers acted as mediators and attempted to facilitate a reconciliation. This seldom happened and the teachers were pleased to note that in the final project evaluation the pupils rated their sense of ownership of the final product very highly.

During these lunchtime rehearsals a number of pupils began to think about the presentational side of the piece. They expressed concern that the visual impact of the piece could be limited within a large concert hall space. They undertook to enhance the musical composition in two ways:

1   Through the preparation of a large collage that would be constructed in real time as the music played;
2   Through choreographing a dance to accompany the final two sections of the musical composition (portraying the human inhabitation of Dunwich and its eventual decline).

Both of these additional elements were pursued by groups of pupils over the following weeks. It was exciting to see the purposeful and natural way that pupils worked across the often well-differentiated arts subject boundaries as the concert date got nearer.

In the final week of the project the head teacher agreed to set aside two mornings for full rehearsals. These consisted of one hour for technical set-up and then two hours of rehearsal and performance. The second rehearsal was on the day of the performance so all leads and inputs could be labelled and the entire set-up checked before leaving school. Pupils were made responsible for their part of the set-up to ease re-assembly and disassembly at the concert hall. The final performance was given by the pupils at Snape Maltings concert hall as part of a broader celebration of schools' music organised by the Suffolk County Music Service.

What does *Dunwich Revisited* have to teach us about the way in which a geographical understanding of our locality can help inform a creative process of curriculum development? We think that there are three main points to consider.

1 Developing artistic responses through geographical, historical and cultural metaphors is a powerful way to connect pupils with their locality

Many of the pupils knew about Dunwich and its changing geography. They had visited the coastline itself and explored its various elements. They had studied coastal erosion, something that is a current concern along much of the East Anglian coastline, and were familiar with how the coastline has changed significantly in recent history.

Second, the historical context was important. Pupils had studied the history of the 1832 Reform Act which abolished the rotten boroughs. Up until that time, despite being under water, Dunwich had returned two members of parliament to Westminster! People would travel to Dunwich, take a boat out to where (roughly) the town hall used to be and cast their vote there!

Culturally, the story of Dunwich and its associated myths and folklore were things that many pupils had heard. The idea of standing on the cliffs at midnight with a full moon and hearing the bells toll from the numerous Dunwich churches certainly caught their imagination. Seeing and hearing from the artists first-hand how these contexts had affected existing art works became an important stimulus for the pupils' own artistic processes and thinking.

These geographical, historical and cultural inferences all inspired the pupils to play with musical and visual materials through metaphorical and creative process. They facilitated song writing, physical theatre and dance as well as the production of new compositions that the pupils were able to perform. They also reinforced key learning in geography, history and religious education.

2 Pupils' artistic and musical voices can be empowered in the local context

One of the key working principles within *Dunwich Revisited* was to place a strong degree of emphasis on the pupils' own artistic expression and the promotion of their own musical forms of expression. Despite the decision to present pupils with a wide-ranging amount of initial stimulus materials, as well as an overall structure for the final performance piece, pupils still felt that it was a strong expression of their own emotions and feelings for the place of Dunwich. During interviews, pupils commented:

> Everyone had the chance to contribute. The piece was different and individual. We composed it and no one had heard it before.
>
> (Anna, Year 8, in interview)

> I liked how original and contemporary it is. I mean, there is no other piece quite like it and you could never play the exact same piece again.
>
> (Carla, Year 9, in interview)

In this sense, the framework that underpinned pupils' work within *Dunwich Revisited* acted like a doorway through which they were empowered to create a language of expression that drew on a range of art forms including music, the visual arts, dance and drama. It is hard to overestimate the importance of the physical place of Dunwich in the generation of this curriculum and the responses that the pupils made to it. The pupils' locality is ingrained into their sense of being. It provides a unique space within which their own artistic voices can begin to emerge, be nurtured and be challenged through a skilful and responsive curriculum design.

3 Cross-curricular approaches provide a vital broader curriculum framework for an area-based curriculum approach

Although *Dunwich Revisited* was initially conceived as a musical project that drew on a particular area of Suffolk, it quickly became cross-curricular in its scope. Pupils responded to the ideas being presented and used them to develop a language of expression that spanned many art forms, including music, dance, poetry and the visual arts. On reflection, it seems that the process of starting with the language of the artist itself, of developing the broad curriculum contexts alongside this in the early stages of the project, and of valuing the language of the pupils facilitated, for many involved, a natural engagement with cross-curricular ways of thinking.

Dunwich Revisited was developed almost entirely through the curriculum time available for Key Stage 3 music within the school, together with some related extra-curricular activities. Despite this, there were a number of examples of pupils making cross-curricular links quite naturally. The first of these developments happened early on in the project. The words that were written by a group of Year 8 pupils (see the opening of Case Study 3) became an integral component for a song which formed the centrepiece of the final performance. The language of poetry, as noted by Abbs (2003, p. 13), is closely related to the language of music. Second, during the contemporary dance track performed by a DJ which formed part of the middle section of the piece, pupils were concerned that the performance lacked visual impact. They were quick to suggest the inclusion of dance which, as they commented, 'added an extra ingredient to the piece; it made the piece stand out and made the audience look up and think of the three Dunwich stages shown' (Sue, Year 9). Pupils were also quick to ascribe a meaning to such an activity:

> It brought the mixing alive and represented fun and enjoyment during the daytime in Dunwich.
>
> (Claire, Year 8, in interview)

> The dancers represented human activity and life, whereas the first and last sections represented nature on its own.
>
> (Chloe, Year 10, in interview)

Finally, alongside the musicians and singers a collage was assembled, piece by piece, as the performance took place.

It is important to stress that the inclusion of poetry and song-writing, dancing and the accompanying collage were ideas generated by the pupils themselves. Unlike the curriculum planning that underpinned Case Study 2, these connections were quite unexpected to the teachers – but celebrated and encouraged! To conclude this discussion of *Dunwich Revisited*, the following extract from the journal kept by one of the teachers involved in running the project re-emphasises some of the points made above:

The naturalness in which the pupils made connections across the art forms is a real challenge to my way of thinking. The nature and structure of the curriculum within our high school does not actively facilitate the making of these links across the arts curriculum. In many respects the boundaries are well and truly established and maintained. But in contrast to this, pupils were more than happy to translate their ideas within a number of differing artistic contexts with great success. I believe this happened because in their wider lives pupils do not isolate artistic practices into discrete units of experience.

Case Study 3 explored how the geography of a place, Dunwich, inspired a music project that quickly turned into an arts project and resulted in a celebratory and original piece of music that pupils valued highly.

The final two case studies in this chapter are from the work of a highly esteemed English educator, David Stevens. They recount two approaches to the use of specific localities as a starting point for curriculum development. As you read them, consider these key elements that characterise an area-based approach to geography curriculum development:

1   Inspiring pupils' interest in their local area's physical and human geography;
2   Considering how a location's natural resources, people and industries work together to produce a sense of space and place in the local community;
3   Developing an appreciation of how a physical location, together with the human interactions that have taken place with and within that location, have changed and developed over time;
4   Representing through artistic and creative responses how a locality is situated both at a fixed point and over a period of time;
5   Comparing and contrasting these things with other locations and environments;
6   Applying knowledge, skills and understanding developed through an appreciation of one's own locality to other areas of the country and the wider world.

Case Study 4 Teaching Brian Friel's *Translations*

Set in late-nineteenth-century Ireland, the play *Translations* imaginatively explores the relationship between language and power through the device of showing how British imperialist ambitions depended on the (apparently innocent) project of remapping the terrain, and in the process (not quite so innocently) renaming Irish localities and (blatantly not innocently at all) quelling any rebellion. My own enthusiasm for teaching this text, apart from its literary and humane qualities, has much to do with a personal fascination with maps – a fascination which to my delight has been shared by some pupils. ... The scope of the play actually goes well beyond the theme of maps (to include cultural identity, education, social mobility and romance across boundaries), but the subject of mapping and its language(s) is fundamental: hence the title. The possibilities for inventive interdisciplinary teaching and learning here seen endless; a selection might include:

Historical or cultural contextualisation:

•   Brainstorm ideas on and impressions of Ireland, contrasted to England, Wales, Scotland or wherever;

- Directed research activities on aspects of Irish culture;
- The Irish dramatic tradition – Yeats, Synge, O'Casey, Behan *et al.*;
- Investigation of media presentations of Ireland, past and present.

Language and communication:

- Investigation of the relationship between languages and imperialism;
- Language, dialect and cultural/national identity;
- The nature of translation, interpretation and connotations;
- The associations and characteristics of the featured languages (Greek, Latin, Gaelic, English) and, by extension, other languages;
- The significance of naming in a variety of contexts.

Other possibilities include:

- Active exploration through music and oral culture, making use of the plentiful Irish resources available;
- Focus on the nature of education and schooling, in particular the relationship between learning, subversion and control;
- Exploration of character and stereotype;
- Learning through drama, performance, role play, tableau, etc.;
- Nature of maps and mapping; metaphorical significance and ideas of control;
- Writing tasks, both empathetic and textually analytical.

(Stevens 2011, pp. 89–90)

Case Study 5 Wordsworth and the Lakes

A geographical sense of place certainly may have the effect of transforming the learning experience for English study. I remember early in my teaching career, having signally failed to inspire my first A-level English literature group with study of D.H. Lawrence's *Sons and Lovers*, deciding to drive them in the school minibus to Lawrence's hometown Eastwood, the setting of his largely autobiographical first novel. I had done my homework and I was able to guide them around several key sites, including Lawrence's childhood home, with resplendent lilies in the front garden, and a view of 'Miriam's' home. Study of the novel came to life, and the power of location for teaching English has never left me. As a further example of successful practice, we could consider the scheme of study below; it is based on reading both of text and of landscape – and the practiced eye does read landscape – devised through the collaboration of English and geography teachers to introduce the topic of Wordsworth and the Lake District landscape to Key Stage 4 pupils.

Resources:

- Large-scale, detailed OS map of the Lake District, together with contours and shading;
- Pictures and photographs of the Lakes – past and present, industrial and agrarian, 'realistic' and 'romanticised';
- Extract from biography of Wordsworth and a selection of portraits;
- A selection of A.W. Wainwright's careful line drawings (themselves works of art mingling mapping with landscape) and evocative prose descriptions;

- Extracts from Wordsworth's autobiographical poem 'The Prelude';
- Extracts from Dorothy Wordsworth's *Journal* to match the subject matter of her brother's poems;
- Tourist information literature based on the Lakes, from different periods and representing contrasting presentational styles;
- Other written or pictorial records, such as newspaper articles, National Park information, Dove Cottage information or planning information;
- Extracts from pertinent children's literature (such as Beatrix Potter's tales and Arthur Ransome's *Swallows and Amazons*.

Activities:

- Whole-class work: general discussion on the nature of the resources used, emphasising the different types of 'reading' involved and the contrasting messages conveyed by the various materials. The stress should be on the purpose and context of a range of readings, and on similarities and differences between readers/readings.
- Pairs examine and briefly report back on a particular (chosen) resource in the light of this discussion, with explicit guidelines provided.
- Small-group activity: pairs expand to groups of four or six and work towards representing information from the chosen resources in a different form, making connections across the different types of material in so doing (e.g. magazine article in *Country Living*, or similar in *The Big Issue*, a local community radio programme, a guidebook for a specific readership).

(Stevens 2011, pp. 90–91)

These case studies take us a little bit away from our central context of using one's locality as a stimulus for an area-based curriculum approach (unless you happen to live in Ireland or the Lake District!). However, we have included them because they do represent a particularly vivid and rich approach to the use of a geographical area and its history. Many of the points that we made in respect of the *Dunwich Revisited* case study are pertinent here. But in these case studies notice the emphasis on the sense of place as developed through the authors that have inhabited it and represented it through their writings. These have been used to make constructive links through a cross-curricular pedagogy to many other subject areas including geography, music, drama, history and languages.

The opportunities to visit a place, as in Case Study 5, are highlighted. Clearly, visiting remote places of natural beauty such as the Lake District is going to be expensive and difficult to arrange for the vast majority of teachers. This is one of the significant benefits of drawing on your local area instead! But familiarity with a local area can be a source of difficulty as well as an opportunity. What Stevens is arguing in Case Studies 4 and 5 is that drawing on the ways in which others have interpreted an area in their writings can be a very helpful way of broadening our understanding of that area today. The opportunity to challenge pupils' perceptions of their local area through maps, art, literature, music and other materials that relate to their locality and show how others have perceived it can be incredibly powerful. Perhaps the best exemplification of that approach was described in Case Study 2.

One of the challenges of Case Studies 4 and 5 is that we, as teachers, should be informed and knowledgeable about the locality in which our school is based and within which our pupils reside (even if we live elsewhere). Knowing about the writers, musicians, artists and others who have drawn on that locality in their work is a very important first step. We are used to discussing the importance of subject knowledge in teacher education. Perhaps we also need to start thinking about the importance of 'local knowledge' too? Being able to construct meaningful curriculum projects from this (with or without the involvement of external partners) is an important second step in designing an effective area-based curriculum that draws on the geography of your local area.

Summary

This chapter has considered a range of different approaches to the use of a local area's geography as a stimulus for area-based curriculum development. Through five case studies, we have seen how one should, and perhaps should not, use one's understanding of the geography of a locality to locate and facilitate pupils' learning in different ways. As this chapter draws to a close, it is worth summarising a few important points.

First, using this type of approach to curriculum development does not mean that you have to abandon the notion of teaching an academic subject. Throughout this chapter we have argued that a basic understanding of geography as an academic subject is an important prerequisite in facilitating this approach to an area-based curriculum. However, it is important to remember that you do not have to be an expert in geography, or a geography teacher either, to engage in this approach.

Second (and we hope this will be obvious by now), an area-based approach to curriculum development that draws on a local area's geographical dimensions will not solely be about teaching geography! As we have seen in all our case studies, while these examples of curriculum development all touch on aspects of the geography curriculum (some of them in a very basic way), they all extend outwards from this very rapidly and encompass a very broad range of subject areas.

Therefore, an area-based curriculum development approach of this type is very closely related to a cross-curricular approach to teaching and learning. Elsewhere, this has been defined as follows:

> A cross-curricular approach to teaching is characterised by sensitivity towards, and a synthesis of, knowledge, skills and understandings from various subject areas. These inform an enriched pedagogy that promotes an approach to learning which embraces and explores this wider sensitivity through various methods.
>
> (Savage 2011, pp. 8–9)

There are a number of key words in this statement that reflect the intricate relationship between subject areas and their established cultures and history, and how these relate to the production of a new kind of curriculum development. It does require a *sensitivity* towards traditional subjects, an ability to *synthesise* knowledge, skills and understanding in a creative way from these subjects, and the development of an *enriched* pedagogy that can deliver this type of curriculum to pupils in active and engaging way. It does not mean the demise of these subjects. We will return to these thoughts towards the end of Chapter 5.

In addition to these highly important and foundational points, an area-based approach to curriculum development utilising a geographical dimension will be characterised by the following key elements discussed above:

1   Using an understanding of a local area's physical and human geography to inspire in pupils a curiosity and fascination about their locality;
2   A consideration of how a location's natural resources, people and industries work together to produce a sense of space and place in the local community;
3   An appreciation of how a physical location, together with the human interactions that have taken place with and within that location, have changed and developed over time;
4   The opportunity to represent through artistic, creative and metaphorical responses how a locality is situated both at a fixed point and over a period of time;
5   The chance to compare and contrast these things with other locations and environments;
6   The ability to apply knowledge, skills and understanding developed through an appreciation of one's own locality to other areas of the country and the wider world.

References

Abbs, P. (2003) *Against the Flow: Education, the arts and postmodern culture*. London, RoutledgeFalmer.

DfE (Department for Education) (2014) 'National Curriculum in England: Geography'. www.gov.uk/government/publications/national-curriculum-in-england-geography-programmes-of-study/national-curriculum-in-england-geography-programmes-of-study [last accessed 28 March 2014].

Harris, R., Harrison, S. and McFahn, R. (2012) *Cross-Curricular Teaching and Learning in the Secondary School: Humanities*. London, Routledge.

RSA (Royal Society for the encouragement of Arts, Manufactures and Commerce) (2012) *Thinking About an Area-based Curriculum: A guide for practitioners*. London, RSA.

Savage, J. (2011) *Cross-Curricular Teaching and Learning in the Secondary School*. London, Routledge.

Savage, J. and Challis, M. (2001) 'Dunwich Revisited: Collaborative composition and performance with new technologies'. *British Journal of Music Education* 18:2, pp. 139–149.

Stevens, D. (2011) *Cross-Curricular Teaching and Learning in the Secondary School: English*. London, Routledge.

Chapter 3

The history of place

Introduction

In these early chapters we are exploring how the different features or characteristics of your locality can be used as a stimulus for an area-based curriculum development approach. This approach is very different from developing a curriculum in response to external factors. We certainly know teachers who make curriculum changes only in light of new national directives or, even worse, changes in GCSE syllabuses. As much as one needs to acknowledge that pupils, at the end of their schooling, have to pass a test, we must consider these as outcomes of our work and not the driving force behind curriculum development. Your curriculum is much more important and powerful than a syllabus.

In Chapter 1, we introduced a definition for an area-based curriculum developed by the RSA. They describe an area-based curriculum as one that is:

- *About* a place: making use of local context and resources to frame learning;
- *By* a place: designed by schools in partnership with other local stakeholders; and
- *For* a place: meeting the specific needs of children and local communities.

(RSA 2012, p. 5)

The objectives of such a curriculum were to:

- Create learning experiences that are engaging for children from all backgrounds;
- Increase children's understanding of and attachment to the place where they live;
- Embed schools more deeply within their communities and localities.

(Ibid.)

In this chapter, we will be drawing explicitly on the first part of the RSA definition (i.e. the locally-based curriculum being *about* a place) and on the second of their key objectives – increasing pupils' understanding of and attachment to the place in which they live.

At the beginning of this book we stated that who and what we are, as authors, was shaped by our own journeys as individuals: where we grew up, whom we grew up with, and our interaction with those places shaped our identities in a number of different ways.

The history of a place is evident in all of our interactions with it. How you park your car, drive to work, commute on public transport or walk your children to school are all shaped by the history of the area in which you live. This history is often very closely linked to key factors of settlement development in that area.

Reflective task

What are the key 'histories' within your local community that have shaped the lives of your pupils? If you yourself are from that area, how have they shaped you?

Understanding history

Although this chapter is not about teaching history, it is important to gain an overview of the broad types of knowledge and understanding that your pupils will have in relation to history, as an academic area for study in school, in order to inform your own understanding of how the history of your local area could helpfully inform the construction of an area-based curriculum approach in your own teaching. As Facer so eloquently suggests, 'the aim of an area-based curriculum is to create rich connections with the communities, cities and cultures that surround them [schools] and by distributing the education effort across the people, organisations and institutions of a local area' (Facer 2009, p. 2).

The National Curriculum contains the following statement about the importance of studying history:

> A high-quality history education will help pupils gain a coherent knowledge and understanding of Britain's past and that of the wider world. It should inspire pupils' curiosity to know more about the past. Teaching should equip pupils to ask perceptive questions, think critically, weigh evidence, sift arguments, and develop perspective and judgement. History helps pupils to understand the complexity of people's lives, the process of change, the diversity of societies and relationships between different groups, as well as their own identity and the challenges of their time.
>
> (DfE 2014)

The National Curriculum presents the aims of ensuring that all pupils:

- Know and understand the history of these islands as a coherent, chronological narrative, from the earliest times to the present day: how people's lives have shaped this nation and how Britain has influenced and been influenced by the wider world;
- Know and understand significant aspects of the history of the wider world: the nature of ancient civilisations; the expansion and dissolution of empires; characteristic features of past non-European societies; achievements and follies of mankind;
- Gain and deploy a historically grounded understanding of abstract terms such as 'empire', 'civilisation', 'parliament' and 'peasantry';
- Understand historical concepts such as continuity and change, cause and consequence, similarity, difference and significance, and use them to make connections, draw contrasts, analyse trends, frame historically valid questions and create their own structured accounts, including written narratives and analyses;

- Understand the methods of historical enquiry, including how evidence is used rigorously to make historical claims, and discern how and why contrasting arguments and interpretations of the past have been constructed;
- Gain historical perspective by placing their growing knowledge into different contexts: understanding the connections between local, regional, national and international history; between cultural, economic, military, political, religious and social history; and between short- and long-term timescales.

(Ibid.)

It is the final bullet point that offers the only reference to 'local' history within the aims. This will be further highlighted and illuminated in our first case study below.

Reflective task

Consider the following two questions:

- What key principles or processes can you take from the statements above, relating to the key understanding, aims and skills associated with the academic subject of history, and how these could be applied to a process of area-based curriculum development?
- To what extent are the principles and processes presented in the above statement suitable as a focal point for planning a new piece of area-based curriculum development?

As you read further through this book it is important to realise the overlapping and interrelated importance of these first five chapters. We believe that there is considerable strength in developing cross-curricular work at the same time as seeking to develop a local curriculum for your school. We would encourage you to do further reading about cross-curricular work (much is available, e.g. Savage 2011), and to evaluate its positives and negatives for your classroom, department and school. As a starting point, we would encourage you to look at what each individual subject offers, not just in the development of knowledge within that subject, but as unique to its way of working. What is it that makes each subject unique in the way in which it is taught, learnt and used as a vehicle for learning? We suggest this as a starting point for developing cross-curricularity rather than just looking at how basic knowledge can be shared through specific projects that you might design.

The first case study in this chapter is a review of the Key Stage 3 history curriculum at Copleston High School on the outskirts of Ipswich in Suffolk. It emphasises how the development of a locally-based curriculum can help develop high motivation in both pupils and staff and give the pupils a very real insight into who they are and why their local area is important to them.

Case Study 1 Copleston High School

Copleston High School is a mixed comprehensive school for pupils aged 11 to 18 on the outskirts of Ipswich, Suffolk. The key to history's success in this school is the innovative nature of the outstanding Key Stage 3 curriculum. It is a model of excellent practice and ensures that pupils have a good understanding of how the history of the local community fits into wider British, European and world history. It has been informed by the teachers' determination that history should be meaningful and relevant to all groups of pupils. Their commitment to recognising, interrogating and celebrating the diversity of the local community is exemplified by the way in which diversity is explored throughout work covered in Years 7 to 9.

Neal Watkin is an advanced skills teacher in history at the school. He commented:

> During the last three years we have had the opportunity to make the curriculum more exciting. We asked pupils what they wanted to do and they were very clear: more local history and investigations which give a more positive view of minority groups. We also wanted to reflect the very diverse population in the school. So we centred our revised curriculum on the pupils' experiences and included much more local history.

Roberto Iacobucci, the head of history, commented that:

> Quite simply, the history we teach is built around our pupils and we use local stories to reveal the bigger picture. We are always looking for other local angles because it is the local connection which makes all the difference.

Throughout the year, each half-term topic is rooted in a local theme: e.g. the enquiry on 'How did the Norman invasion affect Suffolk?' centres on an investigation of Framlingham Castle. Through research on why the castle was built, when it was built and where it was built, pupils move on to see to what extent the experience of this part of Suffolk was representative of what happened elsewhere in England. In this way the local community experience is used as a micro study – how was this part of Suffolk affected? – of a macro issue – how was England affected as a whole? This opportunity for pupils to move seamlessly from local history to national history and back to local history again goes far to explaining why the curriculum in this school helps to strengthen their chronological understanding.

All the units are devised in the same way. Another example can be drawn from the question 'How successful was Elizabeth I at overcoming the problems she faced?' Pupils begin with a local perspective. In this case, it is Elizabeth's progress to Kentwell Hall in Suffolk. An enquiry into what happened on the royal progress, and more importantly why she made it, broadens out to look at the problems Elizabeth had to deal with and the extent to which she overcame them. Again, the pupils move from the local event to the national scene, shaping and reshaping their views as their enquiries develop.

In the case of Thomas Clarkson, the pupils interrogate not only the local impact of his work but also his national and international importance. Thomas Clarkson's contribution to the movement for the abolition of the slave trade has been to a large extent eclipsed by that of his better-known colleague, William Wilberforce. However, Clarkson played a pivotal role in arguing the case for abolition. In their studies, pupils are linking not only from the local to the national scene but also to the international landscape. They look at how famous people are remembered, focus on how Clarkson has been commemorated and finally consider how he should be commemorated. They develop trenchant views on his importance and much disgust at the inadequacy, in their view, of his current commemoration. As one pupil commented, 'More people need to be aware of Thomas Clarkson and what he did and it is up to us, the young people, to do that.'

Although local history is central in Year 7, it is also integrated into topics studied in Years 8 and 9 and the curriculum is peppered with references to the local context. For example, in Year 8, pupils study the civil war in East Anglia. In Year 9, the themes of how conflicts should be remembered are focused on the part played by the Suffolk and the Royal Anglian Regiments both in the two World Wars and since 1945.

Putting the local community at the heart of the history curriculum at Key Stage 3 has also led to a detailed study of issues of diversity throughout the units covered. While the large majority of pupils at the school are of White British heritage, the department is keenly aware that some pupils are not. They are determined that history should be highly relevant to everyone in the school and this is reflected in a curriculum which ensures that issues regarding diversity are built into the curriculum rather than treated as tokenistic add-ons.

The work on diversity is brought together in Year 9 with a separate project on the 'Ipswich Caribbean Experience' as part of the general enquiry question, 'How should the twentieth century be remembered?' Pupils engage in a project to save the Ipswich Caribbean Association building. As part of this study, they explore migration through time and the impact of the Caribbean community on Ipswich as well as the impact of Ipswich on the Caribbean community itself. Again it is a local perspective that leads the pupils to investigate a broader issue, from the experience of the Ipswich Caribbean community to the wider theme of migration at a national and international level. Pupils find this unit fascinating, not least because they come to understand much more why people are so prepared to move across the world no matter what the difficulties.

For Roberto Iacobucci and all his colleagues, the curriculum has brought greater levels of engagement and motivation among pupils. As a result of this work, more families, most of whom have children at the school, are visiting Christchurch Mansion in Ipswich, the focus of a unit in Year 7 on religious changes in Tudor England, and Playford Churchyard, just outside the town, where Thomas Clarkson was buried.

By the end of Year 9, pupils have not only a detailed grasp of the topics and themes they have studied but also an in-depth understanding of why history matters to them. The exemplary curriculum at Key Stage 3 ensures that they can confidently articulate the place history has in their own lives, in society and in the modern world. In the words of one pupil, 'The history we study helps you to see where you fit in and why we do what we do'. Another agreed and added, 'Yes, and I now know who I am'. (Ofsted 2011, edited from pp. 1–5)

Reflective task

There are clear ideas here that are worth investigating further as we develop our thinking about how a historical approach can embrace and develop an area-based curriculum. It is a combination of several factors that makes the locally-based history curriculum at the school a success. These are not unique to this school. What elements can be picked up and used to help develop an area-based curriculum at your school which brings alive your local history?

For us, there are three main points that we would like to consider drawn from this case study.

1 The centrality of outstanding teaching

It is clear from the case study that the teaching in the history department is very good. But what makes it so? As experienced teachers we know that there are many ways in which teachers can be outstanding and deliver lessons that motivate and engage their pupils. Although there are no set rules for being an outstanding teacher there are several key characteristics that outstanding teachers normally have.

From the pupils' perspective, outstanding teachers have a love and passion for their subject. This is clear in everything they do. When we ask pupils about these things, they also mention that their outstanding teachers are well prepared and organised, and this helps in the flow of lessons. They also, and perhaps most importantly, mention that they care about them as individuals, they help them understand who they are and they make links between their schoolwork and their broader development as young people.

It is important, then, to ask how the development of an area-based curriculum supports this work by the teachers in the history department at Copleston. How does it enable them to deliver good and outstanding lessons? It is important to see Stenhouse's link again between curriculum and teacher development. Although the teachers talk directly of how the local history curriculum inspires the pupils and their families and helps them develop a greater appreciation of the town in which they live, the argument is clearly reversible. The teachers themselves are being inspired to look for new catalysts in the local area that can inspire their work; they are on a journey of discovery about their subject, how it can be delivered and how this is enriched by drawing from what is closest to them.

As the teachers work in this way, they develop their own subject knowledge and become greater experts on the area in which they live. Even in what can seem the most barren of 'historical' areas, they will find engaging points of departure for curricular activities. Pupils will make amazing discoveries; they become active historians, rather than just pupils who know some historical facts. This will form part of their cultural heritage that they may have never considered and will bring to life the area in which they live.

There is greater argument about context here also. Some of our most inspirational memories of teachers, from all our school days, were teachers who were able to make the work fit into a 'real' context. We were inspired by lessons that seemed to sit within a context that was outside of the classroom in which we worked. In one local project recently, pupils were asked to compose a piece for a local event, a real event, to commemorate the local football legend Sir Stanley Matthews whose statue was to be unveiled in the city centre high street. Why was this so important? Like the history curriculum at Copleston, it was the first time that music became a 'real' subject for those pupils, one that had a place in their lives, in an area and in the history of Stoke as a town.

2 Strong and determined leadership

The second key lesson from the above case study is that strong and determined leadership can have a major impact on developing an area-based curriculum development. Strong leadership will allow teachers to take risks in what and how they choose to teach. There is a clear sense here that the subject leader has a sense of what is needed by the National Curriculum but an understanding that allowing the teachers to develop this in the local context and deliver this in their own way will benefit all involved.

The leadership at Copleston High School realised this and enabled the staff within the department to make a clear and strong distinction between what should be taught and how it should be taught. They conceptualised the National Curriculum for History as a skeleton structure for the school, something that teachers and pupils would need to put the curriculum 'meat' onto. It was something within which the 'local' became a driving force and took central importance. This distinction has always been there but it is often lost in a focus on attainment or results. It is all too easy to 'teach to the test' or develop only what can be tested; sometimes what counts can't be counted, and what can be counted doesn't count.

It is at the moment of curriculum design that teachers need to make choices about what is important. The National Curriculum's aims for your subject need to be linked to what you feel is important, what other local partners might consider is important, and then placed within a vehicle for learning that has relevance to your subject. Your local area can become the key mechanism that links National Curriculum requirements with the lives of your pupils.

3 Critical thinking

Using the local area can be one of the richest ways to develop critical thinking in our pupils from an early age. What is critical thinking? Put simply in this context, it is about pupils gathering and interpreting knowledge and understanding of the history of their local area. This could be done with any age group and by a variety of means. We could use traditional historical evidence or new technologies to research and collect new data. Critical thinking allows them to interrogate, to form new ideas and opinion and to back these up with facts and data from the local area.

Practical task

Reconsider the general points you drew together in response to the last reflective task. Think specifically about your current curriculum and where it does or could draw from the local history of your area. What 'new' knowledge or data could the pupils discover or create for themselves? How could this be used to develop critical thinking about the subject, history, the local area and themselves? Thinking about a lesson that you are going to prepare, draw these ideas together within a short classroom activity.

Implications for your work

What are the implications of all this for your work as a teacher?

1 Starting local

From the case study a clear point could be the pupils and their understanding of what they wish to study. We might want to start by looking at the earliest settlements in our area. Examining why certain areas were picked over others, your geography teachers will give you good clues to food, water and suitable building land to get you started (see Chapter 2 for further ideas). Getting beyond this, though, we come to the development of villages, towns and cities. This development, often based on the local industries, will have shaped the size, design and evolution of your local area. These, in turn, will shape how you and your pupils live your lives on a daily basis. Wherever your school is based you will find a different process of development here that you can draw upon.

For example, if you live an area which has houses ranging up to 150 years old there will be a drastic change in how the houses are set out, not just internally but in also relating to how they interact with each other as buildings. This will often reflect the local history. In many northern mining and cotton mill towns, early-twentieth-century houses reflected the close communities in which people worked. People not only worked together but lived closely together too.

As we draw from the local history of the place in which we live we need to develop this sense of connection. The pupils in our classrooms are a part of the history, which is not just something that happened in the past; the consequences are rippling through their present experiences too. Pupils recognise this. Pupils at Copleston High School expressed it like this:

> 'The history we study helps you to see where you fit in and why we do what we do'. Another agreed and added, 'Yes, and I now know who I am'.
>
> (Ofsted 2011)

They live in the history of the area but they are an integral part of it too.

2 Working within and beyond subject boundaries

One of the important things that an area-based curriculum approach can develop is the opportunity for pupils to see themselves as more than just a group of people that are on the receiving end of a packaged curriculum. Pupils all develop differently. As teachers we know, though, that certain generalisations and stereotypes about pupils enable us to plan our curriculum to best suit, in a general sense, the pupils we have to teach.

But pupils are complicated! They have very unusual ideas. Ask them what they think school is for, what it 'gives' them or why they have to go? Schools are oddly organised places where subjects, teachers, pupils and buildings are often juxtaposed in confusing ways.

Reflective task

Think about how a typical school organises itself from the perspective of a Year 7 pupil. Contrast this with their experience in a typical primary school, say in Year 6. How was their education organised there? How much time did they spend with a specific teacher? What would they have listed as the priorities in their education? What is important to them in Year 7? How is their schooling organised? How long do they spend with each teacher? How as the importance of 'subject' been introduced? Why have 'subjects' become such an important organising principle? Who makes these decisions in your school?

Taking this into account, how might the history of the area in which your school is placed influence the curriculum choices you make? Whatever your subject specialism is there will be a connection to the local history to be made.

It is important that you take time as teacher to think how this model of curriculum development can be used in your own subject. Taking into account all of the important decisions you make as a teacher and the points made earlier in this chapter, what does the curriculum begin to look like that builds from the pupils outward to the local area and its history?

The importance of the selections we make as teachers cannot be overlooked, though. The selection of curriculum can make a very important link between the pupils and how they are part of the history in the area. As teachers we know that pupils often struggle to see anything that is outside of them as individuals. The school pupil is an egocentric beast, who often interacts with the world on a 'what's in it for me' basis.

3 Building from diversity

In the area where one of us lives, the houses and history very much reflects the two major local industries: coal and cotton. At one time, this small town had seven train stations serving the mine heads with little more than two square miles to cover them all. As the coal industry declined, cotton mills took over. These were not just places to work but grew to such a scale that they became their own 'mini' towns. Housing and infrastructure developed around these and they played a key part in how the history of the place in which we live might shape our futures.

The landscape and people within it are now changing at an even faster pace. The world's population has never seen a time of greater mobility and this does not seem to be stopping. It has become increasingly important to recognise the diversity of our local areas in the school curriculum itself. What diversity is there in my classroom and how is this reflected in the curriculum? Facer has an interesting perspective:

> A curriculum that tells tales of its local communities, then, is not a neutral representation of that environment, but has the capacity to shape, influence and reshape those communities in turn. Who gets to tell the stories about the community, and the types of stories that are told are therefore fundamentally political questions that cannot assume the rights of one group to name and represent the area for all other groups.
>
> (Facer 2012)

Reflective task

Take a moment to conceptualise the contribution that parents might make to your curriculum. What knowledge and skill base could they bring? More importantly, how could you draw on their experiences, and who and what they are, to make the connection between school and the pupils' lives stronger? How do families who have lived in the area for several generations see the changes that are happening? Do they consider the changes to be positive or negative? Do they feel included by how this is reflected in school? Consider new families to the area. Do they understand the history of the area, how it developed, why this is important? How can your school help in connecting the local community, history and people together?

The school's link to adults within a local community are vitally important as you seek to build an area-based curriculum. First, adults have significant influence in the lives of their children outside of the school gate. Their attitudes to the world in which they live, the experiences they have and how these are passed on to their children, all frame the work we do with them within school.

Second, parents and other adults influence how the pupils interact with the school itself. Some adults take a very active role in their pupils' education, some will ask very little about what happens during the day in school, but all of this will influence how the pupils work. The adults are the living history in the area; they will tell the stories and share the knowledge of the local area with the next generation. As the local population changes, the stories and rich history that will have been brought with it will take new and more complex routes. The pattern of the local tapestry will become more richly woven.

A curriculum which builds from the pupils outwards to the local community will be best placed to understand the true diversity of the classroom. Rather than seeing any issues of diversity falling at the feet of the pupils, it puts the issue within the wider setting and positions the pupil in a position of power and understanding. This key movement away from an approach that perceives pupils as lacking knowledge and understanding, and towards one that positions pupils at the centre of an empowering curriculum, is one of the greatest benefits of an area-based curriculum.

Summary

On a daily basis, pupils, staff, the school and the community are shaped by the history of the locality. As we have discussed above, there may be many ideas you can draw from in your area. There is a real opportunity today to seize the opportunity to make a truly local, area-based, curriculum within our schools. We would argue that this will not weaken the National Curriculum but rather strengthen its key themes by placing pupils at the heart of the curriculum development process.

It is important to keep in mind our three-tiered definition from the RSA. First, an area-based curriculum is *about* a place, making use of local context and resources to frame learning. As we have discussed, the place in which our school is set is strongly influenced by the history of the surrounding area. The lives of our pupils, their parents and other members of the community are all imprinted with the hallmark of their locality. We have to acknowledge this and seek to understand it fully if the curriculum that our school offers, and the activities that we design and deliver within our teaching, are going to make their mark too.

Second, the RSA remind us that an area-based curriculum is *by* a place: it is designed by schools in partnership with other local stakeholders. As we look into the history of our local area, we have recognised the importance of these key stakeholders. We have already briefly discussed the influence of adults and their attitudes, but we need to consider which other partners and local stakeholders are important. We will be turning our attention to this very important broader network when we consider partnership working in more detail in Chapter 8.

Finally, the RSA definition tells us that an area-based curriculum model is *for* a place; it should meet the specific needs of children and local communities (RSA 2012, p. 5). After reading this chapter, we hope you have some clear ideas of how this has been done and how you could start to develop your own curriculum infused with historical elements drawn from your locality.

As a final point, it is also important to remember the concept of the 'hidden curriculum':

The idea of the hidden curriculum is a reminder that there are things learnt in school that are not identified on the timetable … the way teachers talk to pupils or the habits and behaviours that are drummed into pupils through the routines of the school day.

(Mercier 2013, p. 95)

Schools represent a set of collective values, which are both drawn from and help support society and our interactions with each other as a whole. Education is about something far more important than preparing pupils for the future world of work. Connecting the school to the history and people of the area can help make these broader processes of education far more real and can also help establish a common bond between schools and local communities within which young people are truly 'grounded' (in every sense of that word).

As we have considered throughout this chapter, drawing on the history of our local area it is not always a straightforward thing to describe. Communities and places are forever changing, 'neighbourhoods are not static – they are changing, dynamic, and sites of resistance and colonialism' (Lavia and Moore 2009). The local history of any place is shaped by the people who interact with it; so too the development of an area-based curriculum.

This curriculum approach acknowledges that history can be represented in different ways; the interaction between the curriculum and a locality is constantly shifting and changing as teachers and pupils engage with it through their daily lives. If pupils can see that how they learn is more closely linked to who and what they are as people, they will resonate with it more readily, and meaningful and lifelong learning will result.

References

Comber, B. (2009) 'Critical Literacies in Place: Teachers who work for just and sustainable communities'. In Lavia, J. and Moore, M. (eds) *Decolonising Community Contexts*, London, Routledge.

DfE (Department for Education) (2014) *National Curriculum in England: History*. www.gov.uk/government/publications/national-curriculum-in-england-history-programmes-of-study/national-curriculum-in-england-history-programmes-of-study [last accessed 3 April 2014].

Keen, A. (2012) *Digital Vertigo: How today's online social revolution is dividing, diminishing and disorienting us*. London, Constable and Robinson.

Lavia, J. and Moore, M. (eds) (2009) *Cross-cultural Perspectives on Policy and Practice: Decolonising community contexts*, London, Routledge.

Mercier, C., Philpott, C. and Scott, H. (2013) *Professional Issues in Secondary Teaching*, Sage Publications Ltd., London.

NAHT (National Association of Head Teachers) (2011) *The National Curriculum: Way beyond just knowledge*. www.naht.org.uk/welcome/news-and-media/key-topics/curriculum/national-curriculum-way-beyond-just-knowledge [last accessed 4 April 2014].

Ofsted (Office for Standards in Education, Children's Services and Skills) (2011) *Putting the Local Community at the Heart of the Key stage 3 History Curriculum: Copleston High School*.

RSA (Royal Society for the encouragement of Arts, Manufactures and Commerce) (2012) *Thinking About an Area-based Curriculum: A guide for practitioners*. London, RSA.

Chapter 4

The culture of place

> Schools remain the single most important place where children learn about
> Cultural Education.
>
> (DCMS 2012, p. 8)

Introduction

This chapter will explore how the cultural aspects of place can be used to inform a
process of curriculum development within your teaching. Recent reports commis-
sioned by the government have focussed on the importance of cultural education
(DCMS 2012), and we will be picking up on key themes from this report, showing
how local cultural activities – architecture, digital arts, theatre, film, galleries – can
impact on curriculum development. Examples will be drawn from local communities
around Greater Manchester.

Culture, like many other things that make up our school curriculum, is an ever-
changing combination of knowledge and experience. Knowledge within school is
conceptualised in various different ways. It could be knowledge that relates to curriculum content, e.g. the National Curriculum or a GCSE specification, or it could
be knowledge that relates to other sources of authority within the school and its
local community. Over time, a shared view of what we think it is important for children to know has developed across the United Kingdom. However, it is important to
recognise that this process of selecting what is, or is not, important has consequences
for the organisation of our education system and your school's place within this.

Stenhouse (1967) argued that there needs to be a 'community of educated people'
who make decisions about what is or is not important in the canon of knowledge
within a school. Pring (1995) took this further; while working with Stenhouse's
ideas, he saw this potential educational problem:

> How can we seriously address the aspiration of secondary education for all, irre-
> spective of age, ability and aptitude, where we are deeply rooted in a tradition of
> liberal education which seems accessible only to an academic few? How can the
> best that has been thought and said be made available to young people whose
> interest in, and talent for, literature and the arts and history seem so limited?
> How can they be invited into the house and made to feel at home, not simply
> being forced to press their noses against the window, without the whole educa-
> tional enterprise being trivialised?
>
> (Pring 1995, p. 127)

Elliot, drawing from ideas developed in working with Stenhouse, defined the problem in secondary school as this: 'How can everyone be made to feel at home in the house of culture?' (Elliot 1998, p. 127). They believed that access to this 'house' of culture within school can be very difficult for many pupils. The perceived elitism promoted by a curriculum that values some knowledge above others creates a very real barrier that is almost impenetrable.

This debate continues to be current and topical. What constitutes the 'canon of knowledge' was deliberated extensively in the preparation of the most recent National Curriculum (2014), with allegations of direct political interference by some ministers in certain subject areas. Most teachers would agree that there is a shared agreement within many subjects of great figures, discoveries, events, works, dates and knowledge that could be drawn upon to derive the make-up of the curriculum content. Even with what seems, at first glance, slimmed down national curriculum documents, the devil is in the detail. Civil servants, far removed from your school, area and pupils, have made final decisions about what the central canon of knowledge should be within the National Curriculum.

How this is constructed, interpreted and delivered, though, is still going to be the bread and butter of the curriculum makers, the teachers. What decisions can you really make and how can you make sure that you draw upon what will interest and engage your pupils? How does the culture of your pupils, your local area and its heritage filter its way through the life of your school and the curriculum that you offer your pupils?

Reflective task

Take a little time to consider what you think culture is and how this is represented in your local area. Consider:

• The pupils, both past and present.
• The local area: what is its cultural make-up?
• The local heritage and any specific places of culture.

It may be useful to make this up into a table or diagram that helps you to clarify your ideas.

Defining a cultural education

What is a cultural education? The word 'culture' covers a mass of ideas and knowledge. There are many definitions, some of which will complement each other and others of which seem almost contradictory.

Raymond Williams (1961) defines culture as 'a whole way of life'. Culture and cultural education are the leitmotif of our existence. They are the theme that binds our pupils' existences and ourselves together. The themes in a symphony are revisited, altered and developed over time; they are used to give 'sense' to the listener, to involve them in the music, and to give a sense of recognition even at the first listening. The same is true of culture and its various themes.

In 1982 the United Nations Educational, Scientific and Cultural Organization (UNESCO) World Conference on Cultural Policy came to a view that in its widest sense, culture may now be said to be the whole complex of distinctive spiritual, material, intellectual and emotional features that characterize a society or social group. It includes not only the arts and letters, but also modes of life, the fundamental rights of the human being, value systems, traditions and beliefs.

(UNESCO 1982)

This may seem as quite a challenge, but in essence it challenges us to a focus on how we might help our pupils to gain a better understanding of themselves in their local area and the wider world.

In the National Advisory Committee on Creative and Cultural Education (NACCCE 1999) report *All Our Futures*, cultural education is seen as a key vehicle to foster human creativity and thought:

Young people are living in times of rapid cultural change and of increasing cultural diversity. Education must enable them to understand and respect different cultural values and traditions and the processes of cultural change and development. The engine of cultural change is the human capacity for creative thought and action.

(NACCCE 1999, p. 7)

In European society there has always been a multiple use of the word 'culture' to represent a variety of things in different contexts. In the same way as you will see 'creativity' defined differently, so we come to accept different definitions of the word culture. The NACCCE defines culture as 'The shared values and patterns of behaviour that characterise different social groups and communities' (ibid., p. 48). So, cultural education should encourage and promote the understanding of different groups of people, of individuals and of oneself. It should combine what is best from the canon of cultural knowledge; it should also draw from what has been created by the people it involves, both in looking back to the past and enabling the creation of the new cultural objects in the future.

It is also paramount as a teacher to consider the age of your pupils. During all times of schooling pupils are developing. They are seeking to find their place in the social group, the class, the school and the world. Culture, especially music, fashion and art can play key daily roles in this development of self-awareness. As pupils grow older it is often easy to spot the cultural influences that are acting upon them. Their clothes, friends and social groups will often be very linked to their interests and the culture which they choose to involve themselves with in school and the wider world.

Henley's review (DCMS 2012) includes three particular elements that he considers important in a cultural education:

- The first is knowledge-based and teaches pupils about the best of what has been created (for example great literature, art, architecture, film, music and drama). It introduces them to a broader range of cultural thought and creativity than they would be likely to encounter in their lives outside of school.
- The second part of Cultural Education centres on the development of analytical and critical skills, which additionally have a direct relevance across

other subjects outside the scope of this Review. This is especially important in heritage and history, where the subject could otherwise be reduced to the accumulation of facts, rather than also including the acquisition of an understanding of historical context.

- The third element of Cultural Education is skills based and enables pupils to participate in and to create new culture for themselves (for example designing a product, drawing, composing music, choreographing a production, or making a short film).

(DCMS 2012, pp. 14–15)

It is important as a teacher to consider how these three ideas can be combined into the curriculum and form a skeleton or framework to use for development. As in most school-based activities, it is important to consider where your pupils are in their cultural journey and what they encounter in their everyday lives. What is culture to them, and what is therefore going to be a new encounter or way of thinking? It is vital to celebrate the uniqueness of your pupils and school. It is a time when schools in the same area can and probably should have very different cultural curricula.

It is also vital to balance the acquisition of knowledge about culture against the transferable skills that can be uniquely developed by an engagement with, and deeper thinking or exposure to, new cultural ideas. Cultural context is vital in every subject. In schools where subjects are often the centrepiece of any organisational structure, e.g. the driving force behind the construction of a timetable, there is a clear chance to develop working practices which can be enhanced by cross-curricular thinking if not always cross-curricular working.

Reflective task

Revisit the previous reflective task and the table or diagram you made to represent your ideas. Onto this map, add the knowledge, skills and understanding related to your own subject. How do these interrelate with your initial ideas about culture and how these are represented in and around your school? You may want to do this for a few subjects. This could be developed into a task for a group of teachers who are looking to see how cultural education can strengthen bonds in the curriculum.

Your engagement with these reflective tasks will hopefully give you some ideas of what new skills could be developed by new ways of working. We would encourage you to take seriously our suggestion of working with other teachers (although we know that time is often limited). The group dimensions of a culture education are recognised in many policy documents. In this quote, for example, the DCMS is primarily talking about pupils but we believe that the same points apply to teachers too:

It is important to note that, when delivered well, Cultural Education should not just be about visiting museums, galleries or heritage sites, or about seeing performances, although all of these remain important parts of the whole package of Cultural Education. Often, Cultural Education activities will be collaborative and will help children to learn how to work together as a team. However, it is essential that children and young people are encouraged to undertake regular solo activities, such as reading books, writing stories, drawing pictures, learning crafts or making music. Over time, they will get better at doing each of these things, as they build up skills and knowledge through repetitive practice. It is important to remember that becoming proficient in these solo activities can have a profound effect on a child's development; they should not be overshadowed by other group or experience based facets of Cultural Education.

(DCMS 2012, p. 15)

The culture of your locality will have many different elements. You may have arts, music, sculpture, dance, and many other facets that, when put together, reflect the combined cultural essence of your local area. These will be represented in and around your school. You will also have the identities, ideas, customs and social behaviours of the people or society your school represents. To put this more simply, you will have the people who make up a cultural representation of your area as a whole and the achievements of these people reflected in their cultural output.

Clearly, each school and local area will have its own mix. It will be vitally important for you to look more deeply around your area to get a real sense of the local culture that your school represents. We will consider this further in Chapter 8 when we pick up the theme of partnership as a key element in developing a local curriculum.

This chapter will present three case studies drawn from schools around Greater Manchester. Following the third case study, we will undertake a cross-case study analysis of key themes and relate these to the chapter's main themes of culture and place.

Case Study 1 North Manchester High School for Boys

North Manchester High School for Boys is a comprehensive school for pupils aged 11 to 16 that specialises in the visual arts and media. The school, which was going through considerable change as it moved into being an academy, agreed to participate in the RSA project in 2009 (RSA 2009a). As reflected in other chapters of this book, it took the drive and vision of at least one teacher at the school to invest in this and see it as a chance to develop new ideas and connect to the culture of their local city, Manchester. The deputy head teacher at the school recognised several chances in this work. They could see the value in in taking on what must have seemed like considerable extra work. They saw a chance to connect to local culture, to make sure that curriculum at the school was relevant to the pupils and the area and to raise aspirations through these connections. The deputy head reflected:

> Relevance and recognition are key motivators and drivers for learning. Too often we ask our pupils to study without the meaning or context that they can appreciate. Using Manchester as our key driver we know from experience that this local curriculum will be an ideal vehicle for developing the competencies and skills that enhance a pupil's abilities to be able to learn. The immediacy of the locality is of interest and value and stimulates pupils to further their involvement.

(RSA 2009a)

The project was called 'What Makes Manchester Great'. During a three-week period, pupils visited key areas of significance within Manchester. They collected a range of audio and visual material, including still digital photos and digital video, during these visits. After these visits had been completed, they were asked to work together to produce a film that presented their discoveries on their journeys with the people and places in Manchester. Approximately 90 pupils were involved in the three-week project.

The project adopted a competency-based approach initially. These drove the learning opportunities within the project and became appreciated by pupils as they progressed.

The five key competence areas were:

- Managing Information;
- Managing Situations;
- Relating to People;
- Managing Learning;
- Citizenship.

Each area had three competence statements; e.g. the Managing Situations competence area were broken down into:

- Show initiative, creativity and entrepreneurial skills;
- Manage your time and unexpected changes in your project well;
- Know how to handle both success and disappointment, reacting to uncertainty.

This facilitated an approach to curriculum design that was not 'subject orientated' but encouraged the subjects and teachers to collaborate within a 'curriculum framework'. The five key concepts allowed the project to be driven by a process-led rather than a product-led agenda. The work that the pupils would take on, their experiences and the journeys they would take through this would become more important than their eventual destination. The journey of discovery about themselves, the area in which they live and what makes it 'great' would have enough intrinsic value in itself.

> As part of the project, the school brokered relationships with a number of key cultural venues across Manchester. The school noted how willing these organisations were in working with the school. Venues included Quarry Bank Mill, the Imperial War Museum, Manchester United Football Club, the BBC, URBIS, the Manchester Velodrome, Manchester Transport, Manchester Metropolitan University, Manchester Fayre, Manchester Town Hall, Manchester Library and the Arndale Shopping Centre.
>
> (Ibid.)

The school managed to bring 'on board' an excellent range of partners who could bring a variety of skills, expertise and knowledge to the project. Crucially, they were also from a range of cultural expertise, types and funding. It is important that the pupils not only see their area represented in these partners but that they also see a range of people involved in them. Clearly, an organisation such as a premiership football club will have quite a different make-up to that of a library or shopping centre.

What these partners were able to do was reflect what culture was happening in the area. These had a great range. The types of culture which would be seen at the Imperial War Museum would be very reflective of the struggle to unite Europe, to accomplish as one, but would also bring forth the suffering involved in war. Shopping centres and football clubs and their grounds would reflect a very different type of pop culture but nonetheless be reflective of the area and the people. The use of what could be seen as less high culture was an excellent access point for the pupils. It is likely that because of their daily interaction with some of these venues they would feel happier and more at ease being involved with them. This could then be used to introduce the pupils to the more challenging underlying elements of culture which football represents and develops.

When the senior management reflected on the project, two key themes came from this. These helped position the work more centrally to the concept of a local curriculum that is driven by, but also servant of, the pupils at the school.

First, this project was 'competence based' and the 'knowledge base' was seen as 'secondary' to this. This project took as its strength the focus on the educational process and not just the outcome.

Second, it was delivered with pupils in mixed year groups. In the same ways that pupils will mix across year groups in many school clubs and activities, a school orchestra being a perfect example, there is not a necessity that school days, weeks or timetables need to be collapsed to work in innovative or collaborative ways. We would argue that if these practices, partners and projects are going to be sustained, schools and teachers will have to look at ways in which working in this way becomes more the norm. There is much evidence to show that progress in education is not as linear and age related as general overviews and policies would have us believe. Many schools are now trailing and using 'vertical form groups' which contain pupils from all year groups represented in school. There is no reason why part of the curriculum could not be made up from projects which are not year-group specific but purposely take advantage of the skills and knowledge that would be developed from working with pupils of different ages.

During this case study, Manchester itself became the focus of the curriculum project. The opportunities that teachers and pupils had to wander around the city and be immersed in its culture, to take photos and videos and to discuss these, were a great experience in themselves. Perhaps you would consider this quite a luxury? We would agree. Not many schools will have the freedom to disband the formal curriculum in this way. However, this access to space outside the classroom is vital in facilitating this deeper form of engagement and learning:

> By allowing and more, facilitating, the space for the pupils to interact outside of the classroom, drawing on the culture of place, person and history around them the teachers and pupils gained a richer a deeper experience that was greater than the goal of the project outcome. The testimonies of the teachers reflect this deeper sense of understanding of the wider context in which the pupils live and develop, and thus a greater importance is placed upon something that is not as easily accountable.
>
> (RSA 2009a)

Again, this was quite a luxury and perhaps is far removed from the circumstances that you are facing in your school. But what was also interesting here is that the teachers' attitudes, skills and ideas were also developed. This approach to working gave the teachers time to interact with the pupils outside of the classroom and also time to think. It introduced them to new parts of the city, to new knowledge and to new skills.

The teachers had to model new skills and new ways of working to support their pupils' development of skills and understanding. All of this combined to give a better understanding of their local culture. It also gave time for the teachers to understand the pupils more as people, to see them in their own environment but having to take on new ideas and skills. It caused one of the evaluators of this project to write the following:

> I was pleased to see that Stenhouse's belief that there is no curriculum development without teacher development is still as relevant in today's curriculum climate as it was in the 1980s (Stenhouse 1980). Teachers today have a vital role in mediating the requirements of the curriculum to their pupils. They are not passive communicators. They are dynamic and responsive agents in mediating and illustrating learning objectives or competencies to their pupils.
>
> (RSA 2009a)

It is easy to set goals of what we want cultural education to be. But as Henley (2012) remarks, it is important not to reduce subjects to just dates, facts and figures but to develop a deeper understanding and context.

The second case study focuses on a competence-based model that was developed at another inner-city Manchester school.

Case Study 2 Parklands High School

Parklands High School, located not far from Manchester's city centre, is in an area called Wythenshawe. Wythenshawe is Manchester's largest district, a mass of houses originally started in the 1920s to alleviate problems of housing and the associated squalor of industrial Manchester.

The school was at the time going through much change; it was becoming an academy and was going through a reworking of its staffing and working procedures. It is an average-sized school with a small sixth form.

The project was seen primarily as a continuation of the school's previous competency programme. The local element of the curriculum, its focus on Manchester, was viewed in two ways – first, as a simple 'hook', a focus for a programme of activity for developing personal, learning and thinking skills; second, as a means of raising pupils' aspiration and pride both in their city and in their own potential (RSA 2009b, p. 2). The project became known as 'Undressing Manchester: The Urban World' and it aimed to achieve the following goals:

- To deliver a curriculum which is broad, balanced and relevant to each individual pupil;
- To create a happy and positive learning environment, fostering mutual respect, consideration for others and personal responsibility;
- To be committed to developing positive relationships with parents, promoting education as a partnership between home and school;
- To establish effective working relationships with other professionals, for the benefit of all at Parklands;
- To promote Parklands as part of the wider community.

(RSA 2009b)

The 'Undressing Manchester' project was designed to fit into a half term's work. The project team designed four interlinking activities. Three of these were to be delivered in school and one involved a whole year group visiting Manchester.

The first activity was an 'Introduction to Manchester'. This linked very clearly to the idea that part of a cultural curriculum should be knowledge-based. The introduction was focused on the pupils knowing more about the culture of the area. This first activity involved three elements:

1   Presentations by some of the staff, enabling them as staff to learn more about the area in order to deliver this to the pupils;
2   Pupils completed individual research work to supplement their own knowledge about the area;
3   Pupils also then shared this in group work.

These activities were based around key themes. The pupils were able to share what they already knew about Manchester, research new knowledge and develop a feeling or understanding of how they were part of the major city on their school's doorstep.

There is of course much to be said for making sure that pupils build upon existing knowledge in any learning activity. There is a sense here that you can build from the pupils as a starting point for curriculum development, what they bring to school and what culture they already know. There is much evidence that this not only makes the learning more relevant but can help the pupils see themselves in the wider context of the local area and Manchester, in this instance, as a whole. As was reflected late in the study, the teachers felt that the pupils in Wythenshawe did not necessarily see themselves as coming from Manchester.

The second activity saw a full year-group of pupils visiting Manchester. This trip involved all pupils from one year group venturing into Manchester in smaller groups. Teachers who were to facilitate the day's activities accompanied them. The guided tours were all given themes that were selected from: Crime and Punishment, Canals, Music of Manchester, Architecture and Green Manchester.

This visit was clearly an ambitious idea set in the context of the school. This 'risk taking' is going to be crucial in any new curriculum development activity. Even though the primary aim of this activity was again linked to personal development and perhaps could have been strengthened with stronger links to cultural development or knowledge, this was a clear underlying theme. Importantly here the setting up of the 'Undressing Manchester' (RSA 2009b) project, a cultural curricular project, gave the space for the teachers to gather 'data' on the pupils in a new and varied environment. This 'data' then allowed them to be critically reflective not only of this project but of themselves and how they would plan for the future. The use of cultural elements within Manchester gave space for the pupils and teachers to interact differently and develop a new sense of belonging to the area.

Activity 3 was a set of master classes:

> Six master classes were each run twice in the course of one day, with 6 groups of pupils taking two different classes. The pupils were allocated to these master classes, which included: graffiti workshop (external artist), clay workshop (teacher), print making (external artist), poetry (external artist), drama (teacher), and music (external artist). The facilitators of these workshops drew on the children's experiences of their visit to Manchester to create a range of cultural artefacts – from group drama pieces to graffiti art.
>
> (RSA 2009b)

These master classes were in the majority supported by outside professionals and gave a chance for pupils to work with new people. Thought and planning here become important and as with many new projects in school, logistical, monetary and child protection issues had to be taken into account. Whether in developing new partnerships, new ways of working or collaborative work with outside professionals these pressures will always be there. We would argue, though, that there would be a far greater gain from this than working in long-established, set routines, which may lack some creative development or input from others. Even when stating similar knowledge, working in similar ways or delivering projects that could be done 'in house' there is a vibrancy and method of working which cannot be replicated. These may not be able to be easily planned for, they will happen with spontaneity and may be surprising outcomes, but none the else may become vital. This is best reflected here by the work with the poet:

> It turned out that the hip hop poetry workshop was the most fascinating one going and you had members of staff hearing about its reputation throughout the day and going in and visiting the workshops which was fantastic because, on the Monday, you'd had this sort of negative viewpoint of, oh, competency takes over everything ... but then, all of a sudden, everyone is like 'who's this [poet] that everyone is talking about?' And then going in and people were coming in on their frees to see the graffiti workshop and sit with the kids.
>
> (RSA 2009b)

The fourth and final activity was an independent project:

> This interconnected series of lessons allowed the pupils to develop their own 'response' to their experiences. Pupils, in groups of two classes at a time, worked to develop an idea of an artefact they wanted to create, either independently or collaboratively, and then worked over several sessions to produce this.
>
> (RSA 2009b)

Further reflections and description can be read in the case study, but what can be developed here is that the bringing together of any project has to be focused and linked to clear initial aims. Although a 'blank page' can seem like the most creative thing to give to pupils it can be daunting and quite challenging too. Clear frameworks, boundaries and expectations can often facilitate much more creative and adventurous work. It would have also been very beneficial to link back to the 'Undressing Manchester' project title and what this could mean for the pupils involved.

So what are the main ideas that came from this project? There are several themes that are brought out at the end of the case study.

I Developing teachers' perception and planning

First, there was a change in the teachers' perception of their own subjects and how they planned for their delivery. When challenged by the notion of a competency-driven curriculum project with Manchester as a theme, the teachers had to develop new ways of thinking and working. They were challenged to set aside what was principally a subject focus in school and deal with different ways of working. They also had to develop new understanding of the culture of the area. They found out new things about Manchester, its history, its richness of cultural ideas. They reconceptualised how both high and pop art were reflected in their city and local environment. The teachers also reflected that the project had encouraged them to think differently about their individual subjects, to be less protective of them. They had begun to make connections with other subjects through this way of working which could be developed in the future, to consider how more central teaching themes can be adopted to enrich the experience of education for pupils, teachers and external partners.

2 Developing teacher and pupil relationships

Second, there was a shift in teacher and pupil relationships that was facilitated by this new engagement with 'the culture of place'. Teachers were clearly concerned about how pupils would deal with the flexibility and opportunities inherent in a trip into Manchester. Yet this was one of the great successes of this project. Not seen just merely as a day out from school, this structured visit allowed teachers to see pupils taking on new responsibilities, ones that they relished, and the pupils rose to the challenge.

> You can see the pictures there, just the closeness really, and the friendship that develops between the staff and pupils when they're outside and I think, also just giving them confidence that they can be in a city, and they can feel comfortable in that city, and that strong message that you heard today that it's your Manchester, it's your city, be proud of it, be part of it.
>
> (Teacher D, RSA 2009b)

3 Developing a sense of pride in one's locality

Third, a raised awareness of and pride in the environment in which they lived, and of their sense of its diversity, was noted in many of the interviews and conversations with teachers and pupils. If school does not take the opportunity to make pupils more aware of their environment, its culture and the people within it, who will? It may only be in projects such as this that some pupils, who could be argued to most need it, will step outside of their usual environment and social group to see the wider society in which they live and learn. Even in this area, so close to such a large city as Manchester, the pupils saw themselves very much in isolation:

> They're not used to seeing lots of different people, from different styles walking down the street, their hair in dreadlocks that are on purpose, or different styles of clothing, because it isn't necessarily accepted here or seen here. It's not multicultural – it's growing – but it's not a multicultural town at the moment. So to go in there and see so many different ethnicities or different cultures that are going on – seeing African dancing in Piccadilly Gardens. I think that's really important to them and to be aware it's only down the road for them really and the fact that some of them have never been there before, and if we don't take them, or we don't make them aware of it, what is there for them to want to go? I think it is quite important that they got to see it and then they got to.
>
> (RSA 2009b)

4 A shared process of curriculum development

Lastly, the teachers stumbled across the idea of the pupils as curriculum developers themselves. Thorough this creative work the teachers gained a confidence to be more willing to allow pupils to shape ideas and have a more meaningful input into not just how they learn but what they might learn:

> The project, then, has stimulated debate within the school about its relationships with its community, with parents, and with pupils and has generated sufficient enthusiasm and engagement amongst teachers and pupils to ensure that these areas will continue to be explored within the new academy framework.
>
> (RSA 2009b)

The third case study is in a school not far from Wythenshawe but represents quite a different area.

Case Study 3 Whalley Range

Whalley Range is a college for girls aged 11 to 18 with a specialism in Business, Enterprise and Sport. The school decided to run a project entitled 'Our Manchester: Our Whalley Range'. A key focus of this curriculum work was for there to be more project and cross-curricular work in Year 7. The project was run

> over half a term at the beginning of 2009 with all Year 7 pupils. The project involved in the region of 10 days curriculum time and staff from RE, History, Geography, Citizenship and ICT. Each class in the year group was assigned a different period of Manchester's history, and they were then required to plan, film and edit a 'documentary' for their chosen period. It led to the production of a DVD by the whole year group on Manchester's history.
>
> (RSA 2009c, p. 2)

The aspirations and focus for the project were clear from the outset and this was clearly a positive. Themes were chosen to support work in each half term. These were:

- Identity, A Museum for Manchester;
- Our Manchester: Our Whalley Range;
- Heroes and Heroines;
- Fit for Life;
- Twenty-first Century Learning.

As in the previous case study, the teachers were keen for pupils to see themselves in a wider community, to see themselves as part of Manchester, and to widen their knowledge base about the great things that have been created in the city in its past.

> We wanted pupils to have ownership of Manchester because a lot of pupils here don't go out at weekends. They don't go out after school. They might be collected, driven home. They don't travel on public transport ... I think it's partly an ethnicity issue. ... we felt that we wanted to make sure that, every half term, there was some kind of trip so the pupils were getting out and seeing things but we wanted

them to feel 'the city belongs to me; I know my city; I know some of the famous buildings in my city; know I can go into some of these things for free', that kind of thing.

(RSA 2009c, p. 3)

Whether planned for or not, at least one teacher realised that the local area and its culture was an excellent way of challenging the pupils at the school to think differently, to know more about their local area and therefore more about themselves and see how this link to local culture and place could widen further pupils' understanding. There is a danger that an area-based curriculum can have a too narrow, too parochial, focus. There is far more strength in getting the pupils to go somewhere new, see new things which are around them on a daily basis but just a little further away. There is a balance here, but in this case study the school was keen to extend their pupils' knowledge of their city outside the immediate vicinity of the school.

The activities in this case study were well planned, linked and thought out so that they could be resourced effectively and professionally. The plans took several different formats but always drew from a linked set of activities that allowed the pupils to develop their learning:

> The model for the Year 7 project days was a combination of whole year group activities in the hall, in which teachers would present a set of materials and activities intended to inspire and challenge pupils before setting them a major project to work on.
>
> This was followed by a series of activities in classrooms and on visits as a class group in which pupils worked through a handbook to structure their activities. Pupils here could be introduced to new skills and ways of working. The teachers linked this very well to the cultural heritage of the pupils at the school. They made sure that the projects and visits challenged stereotypes and facilitated the pupils' involvement in new ways of work.
>
> Each half term led to a different end 'product' created by the pupils. On the Museum for Manchester, they constructed a physical museum model and made a PowerPoint presentation. On the identity day, they created a class exhibition.
>
> (RSA 2009c, p. 4)

Reading through the full RSA case study from Whalley Range, it is clear that a number of key points made this a successful project. First, the clear focus for this project was well supported with various forms of technology that empowered the pupils' engagement with their local area and gave them the tools to reconsider the cultural elements that the project wanted them to focus on. For example, the production of a DVD by the pupils was, at the time, a current and fresh way of working with digital tools that facilitated the production of a new cultural object, i.e. a film, that reflected their own understanding of Manchester's culture.

As in the previous case study, the teachers and pupils were familiar with working in subject groups. Teachers prepared materials, delivered lessons and balanced the cross-curricular elements of the project within this familiar framework. They supported it well with ongoing reflective activities that pupils completed about their projects, so that work could be monitored. Rather than taking cross-curricular work to mean just sharing topics or foci, the teachers really developed new ways to approach key cultural themes, share pedagogies (that were traditionally subject-based) and develop their own teaching styles and approaches in new directions. Clearly, this required an investment of time on the teachers' part, but the benefits were considerable:

> Over the course of the year, increasingly, the team was coming to focus on the skills and competencies rather than the subject content. A new approach was developing, which saw the staff increasingly see the need to pay attention to the skills pupils required to participate in project based work.
>
> (RSA 2009c, p. 6)

It is clear that this year-long project-based approach was very successful. More than just in the success of each individual project, the whole year changed the teachers' and pupils' approach to ways of working within an area-based curriculum approach and developing pupils' understanding of Manchester and its culture.

Key themes of the case studies

In comparing the three case studies presented from the work of the RSA in Manchester, it seems clear to us that there are three main themes that we could consider further, as set out in Table 4.1 and as described in what follows.

I The development of new knowledge

The development of new knowledge about culture was clear in all of the case studies. The visits to Manchester allowed pupils to experience the cultural elements of their local environments in different ways. The third case study is an excellent example of this. Visits were definitely conceptualised as opportunities to enrich the pupils' current cultural awareness.

The visits were facilitated by teachers working with external partners. This worked best when the visits were given a clear focus and educational rationale. The longer duration of the third case enabled the school to reflect much better over time and perhaps give the out-of-school visits more focus and structure. The termly projects allowed time for reflection and thought by all involved and facilitated the teachers' engagement with effective medium- and longer-term planning. This meant that as projects were developed for each term, new knowledge and skills could be thought about and this could be better linked to a visit out of school. A deeper working relationship between teachers and pupils was another key benefit here. The pupils worked with a single teacher for one day a week over the whole year. This allowed teachers and pupils to develop a strong bond. It allowed teachers to better understand their pupils' and the group's needs.

One of the great successes of the second case study was the use of outside professionals to support the master classes within the school. It is important here to note that the culture of your area is not just in the city, in its places and architecture, but also lives in the people who make the city and community come alive. Each school will have a rich resource base of parents, professionals and partners, which they can draw on to help facilitate a similar process. Parents can certainly be the most neglected of these groups, yet they hold the key to a box of cultural delights.

Table 4.1 Three themes drawn from the RSA case studies in Manchester

Key elements	Case Study 1	Case Study 2	Case Study 3
Development of new or key knowledge: the best of what has been created. Introducing pupils to a broader range of cultural thought and creativity than what they would be likely to encounter in their lives outside of school	Three-week project that took the pupils into the local environment to collect video, audio and picture resources	Three-week project that introduced the pupils to Manchester; pupils went on a visit into the city and developed that work in school through master classes	New knowledge presented in each project; this was supported by seeing it in context through visits outside of school
The development of new analytical, critical and creative skills: making the cultural experience more real and deeper than facts and figures	Focused two weeks of visits with reflection and an intense period of work	Master classes that allowed pupils to see and interact with new skills and ways of working	Separate projects that allowed staff and pupils to develop new ways of working; the growing relationship with one group throughout the year supported this
Creating new cultural objects	Short two-minute films to bring together the work of the previous weeks	A carousel of master classes that allowed pupils to develop different responses to the work they had encountered	Several projects, one day per week throughout a year, which joined together into a larger piece of work

2 The development of new analytical, critical and creative skills

In all case studies we can find evidence of pupils being able to develop their thinking from *knowing*, to *engaging with*, and eventually to the development of new *critical and creative* thinking. There is an important requirement here to balance the drive for a knowledge-based curriculum with the development and fostering of creativity. Excellence in cultural education should be a synthesis of these two approaches. Creativity is not an alternative to academic learning. A rounded cultural education should, as argued by Henley (2012), combine creative exploration and the development of knowledge and skills but more importantly give the pupils a sense of who and what they are in any particular time or place. A rich cultural education can help pupils get a better understanding of who they are as a person, how they fit into the timeline of cultural development and change, and how they can influence this in the future. It also gives them a sense of understanding that they are an individual who exists within a particular time and place, a local area, that is an important and informing part of their identity. These are clearly important concepts for all children at a vital stage in their development.

3 Creating new cultural objects

Pupils creating new culture for themselves was an important part of all of the case studies. The longer time period covered by the third case study allowed pupils the time to do this really well. Final products became more focused, were of better quality and were supported by better resources as teachers were more equipped to adjust to their individual groups' needs.

New technologies were employed by all of the schools to help pupils create these final products. Many teachers expressed reservations about this and some were clearly worried that the projects would fail because of their lack of technical knowledge. However, despite an apparent gamble in this respect, in the vast majority of cases this paid off. Pupils and teachers rose to the challenges and produced cultural objects that were rich in meaning and also underpinned by the development of good technical and creative skills. There is a very important lesson in all of this for us as teachers. We must make sure that as we develop new curriculum ideas we are not limited by current practice. Our job is also to produce the classrooms of tomorrow and this will only be done as we gamble a little with new ideas and technologies.

These three case studies give us a rich understanding of how culture can be used to help create an area-based curriculum. It's time to apply some of these ideas to your own work. This chapter will close with a practical task that seeks to do just this.

Practical task

Think about a unit of work that you are going to be delivering over the next few months. Work through the following stages to help redesign the unit with a cultural theme and by using your local area as a resource.

I START WITH CULTURAL KNOWLEDGE

Consider:

- Your pupils. What do they already know?
- Yourself. What do you know already or what skills do you have?
- Your area, the place. What examples are there in the local area that you could use to show the best of its culture?
- Your area, the people. What people, social groups, ethnic groups, professional groups could be used to bring new culture elements to your pupils?

As mentioned earlier, also think about the link between knowing, engaging and developing. Consider:

- *Knowing*: what will the pupils know, what do you want them to know, how does these two dimensions link together?
- *Engaging*: how will the pupils engage with this knowing? How will this engagement develop over time? How can you make sure that this is varied and interesting?
- *Developing*: what new knowledge and skills will the pupils develop? In particular, what new analytical, critical or creative skills can you imagine pupils learning and developing throughout the unit?

2 GET THE LEARNING OBJECTIVES RIGHT

It is vital to consider the learning objectives for your unit and how these are linked to the cultural knowledge that you have explored above. Consider:

- What do you want your pupils to learn?
- How will they learn this?
- Why will they learn it?

Learning objectives have to be selective. Pupils can't learn everything in one go! So, be confident here and prioritise what you think are the most important learning objectives for this unit given its cultural and area-based dimensions.

3 EXPLORE PARTNERSHIP APPROACHES

Building on the work done in step 1 above, are there specific partners you could bring into the planning process for the unit at this early stage? Getting their feedback early on is a very good idea.

As part of the ongoing planning, are there visits you can organise to locations within your local area? Trips to concerts, buildings, museums or any other cultural venue can be pivotal moments in a unit such as this. Don't forget that locations visits are best when they include a mix of high and pop art, balancing an understanding of what pupils may know already and introducing them to something new.

If external trips are impossible to organise for whatever reason, consider approaches that bring new cultural objects or knowledge into the school instead. This is where your external partners can become really useful!

4 PLAN FOR THE CULTURAL OBJECTS THAT PUPILS WILL PRODUCE

What will pupils produce through the unit? Is there a cultural object of some sort that they can create? This might be a film (as in the above case studies), but it could also be a poem, story, picture, sculpture, wall display, newspaper or newsletter article, or anything else that you think pupils might enjoy creating!

5 BE REFLECTIVE BEFORE, DURING AND AFTER THE UNIT

Developing your reflective practice is crucial for all teaching but especially when trying something new. There is a plethora of ways in which this can be done, but it normally involves observing pupils working, having conversations with pupils about their work, writing a journal or keeping notes of sessions, and using all of this as key data to reflect upon in a structured way. The good news is that many of these activities will form part of your day-to-day work as a teacher anyway. What you will need to think through is the formal structure and process of documenting your work in such a way that you can find ways to think differently about your practice and how it is changing as you adopt new pedagogical approaches.

6 PUT THE PUPIL ON CENTRE STAGE

Most importantly, start from where your pupils are. Consider who they are and what knowledge they already bring to school. How can this be enhanced, strengthened and supported by looking at their surrounding culture and cultures? In the end it comes back to Pring and Stenhouse's point, 'how can everyone be made to feel at home in the house of culture?' (Elliot 1998, p. 105). If modern schools are to be truly for everyone, we have to consider how we make everyone 'feel at home'. Our shared understanding of culture, inclusion and learning, and how these are celebrated together within schools and communities, are all shared experiences that have, at their heart, the individual pupil and their well-being.

Working hard at a practical task like this is an important first step in developing a pedagogy that is sensitive to the opportunities of an area-based curriculum. At this point, it is highly likely that you will have many questions about this approach and how it can be developed further in your own and your school's work. We will be considering all of these issues in much more detail in Chapter 6. For now, we are going to turn our attention to the final set of features or characteristics of your locality that you are turning your attention to: community, people and place.

References

DCMS (Department for Culture, Media and Sport) (2012) *Cultural Education in England.* www.culture.gov.uk/publications/8875.aspx [last accessed 29 June 2012].
Elliot, J. (1998) *The Curriculum Experiment.* Buckingham, Open University Press.
Facer, K. (2010) *Towards an Area-based Curriculum: Insights and directions from the research.* London, RSA.
NACCCE (National Advisory Committee on Creative and Cultural Education) (1999) *All Our Futures.* NACCCE.
Pring, R. (1995) 'The Community of Educated People: The Lawrence Stenhouse Memorial Lecture'. *British Journal of Educational Studies* 43:2, pp. 121–145.

RSA (Royal Society for the encouragement of Arts, Manufactures and Commerce) (2009a) *Manchester Curriculum Case Study: North Manchester High School for Boys*. London, RSA.

RSA (2009b) *Manchester Curriculum Case Study: Parklands School*. London, RSA.

RSA (2009c) *Manchester Curriculum Case Study: Whalley Range School*. London, RSA.

Savage, J. (2011) *Cross-curricular Teaching and Learning in the Secondary School*. London, Routledge.

Savage, J. and Challis, M. (2001) 'Dunwich Revisited: Collaborative composition and performance with new technologies'. *British Journal of Music Education* 18:2, pp. 139–149.

Savage, J. and Challis, M. (2002) 'A Digital Arts Curriculum? Practical ways forward'. *Music Education Research* 4:1, pp. 7–24.

UNESCO (United Nations Educational, Scientific and Cultural Organization) (1982) *Mexico City Declaration on Cultural Policies, World Conference on Cultural Policies*. Mexico City, UNESCO.

Williams, R. (1961) *The Long Revolution*. Vintage Books, London.

Wineburg, S., Mosborg, S., Porat, D. and Duncan, A. (2007) 'Common Belief and the Cultural Curriculum: An intergenerational study of historical consciousness'. *American Educational Research Journal* 44:1, pp. 40–76.

Chapter 5

Community, people and place

Introduction

In the opening chapters of this book (Chapters 2 to 5), we are exploring how different features or characteristics of your locality can be used as a stimulus for the development of an area-based curriculum. This chapter will focus on the local community and will explore how curriculum development can be usefully enhanced through models that engage with them in innovative ways.

In Chapter 1, we introduced a definition for an area-based curriculum developed by the RSA. They describe an area-based curriculum as one that is:

- *About* a place: making use of local context and resources to frame learning;
- *By* a place: designed by schools in partnership with other local stakeholders; and
- *For* a place: meeting the specific needs of children and local communities.

(RSA 2012, p. 5)

The objectives of such a curriculum were to:

- Create learning experiences that are engaging for children from all backgrounds;
- Increase children's understanding of and attachment to the place where they live;
- Embed schools more deeply within their communities and localities.

(Ibid.)

Chapter 5 will be focusing on the third part of the RSA definition (i.e. the locally-based curriculum being *for* a place) and will also be considering the third of their key objectives, namely how the curriculum can help embed schools more deeply within their communities. As in the previous three chapters, we will be exploring these themes through a range of case studies chosen from schools' work in this area.

Understanding community, people and place

Unlike the previous three chapters, which took as their starting point a specific academic subject or subjects, the study of 'community, people and place', perhaps through an academic discipline such as sociology, does not appear within the National Curriculum. In fact, the sociological underpinnings of the current National

Curriculum itself are fairly weak when compared to previous versions. Section 2.1 of the current Programmes of Study states that:

> Every state-funded school must offer a curriculum which is balanced and broadly based and which:
> - Promotes the spiritual, moral, cultural, mental and physical development of pupils at the school and of society;
> - Prepares pupils at the school for the opportunities, responsibilities and experiences of later life.
>
> (DfE 2014)

It is hardly a ringing endorsement for a partnership approach and we suspect that the concept of an area-based curriculum has certainly passed by the civil servants who penned this clause! Thankfully, many schools have engaged productively with their communities and, as we shall see from the fascinating case studies below, the benefits of working collaboratively both within and for your local community are numerous.

As in previous chapters, we are going to use case studies drawn from the recent work of schools to illustrate some of the key themes that we want to promote in this book. Our first case study is a straightforward one. It is perhaps the most simple in terms of how a school could make curriculum links with community partners, and provides a number of obvious links with many of the case studies presented in previous chapters. It concerns how one school has worked collaboratively with community partners, including local employers and a university, to construct an art, craft and design curriculum.

Cheslyn Hay High School is a large school for pupils aged 11 to 18 serving Cheslyn Hay and the surrounding area in South Staffordshire, near Walsall. This case study explores how the art, craft and design department at the school developed links with the creative industries and cultural sector. It draws on a case study conducted by Ofsted in 2014 as part of their 'Good Practice' resource database (Ofsted 2014a); the full case study is available on the Ofsted website (Ofsted 2014b).

Case Study 1 Making art, craft and design education relevant to life and work at Cheslyn Hay Community High School

The art, craft and design department at the school makes strong links with the creative industries and cultural sector in order to prepare pupils for a range of subject-related career options and enrichment opportunities. The department has developed a very popular course that secures high achievement by creating real opportunities for girls and boys to experience what it is to be an artist, craftmaker or designer professionally.

One project enabled the pupils specialising in ceramics to redesign an outside seating area at the school. This involved collaboration between pupils, a practising designer and a local brick manufacturer. In preparing their designs, pupils were encouraged to think in three dimensions by drawing on their previous experience of sculpture and ceramics. They gained an insight into collaborative design in response to a commission when their individual ideas for the new seating area were presented, evaluated and eventually combined. A practising designer helped the pupils refine their design.

The department grasps opportunities to work with local industries, in this case an industrial brickmaker, whose processes were used to construct and fire the seating unit. The involvement of this local brick manufacturer deepened pupils' subject knowledge and skills further, in particular when they made moulds for casting at the brickworks. The impact of their work when assembled together was stunning and it has remained a talking point at the school. The seating area is both practical and sculptural. It complements the department's focus on 'creating for a purpose' (ibid., p. 2).

Central to the success of the project was the skilled project management by the teacher specialising in ceramics. Her strong and sustained links with contemporary practice, wide subject knowledge and effective use of continuing professional development created the conditions for the project to succeed. Because pupils' knowledge, understanding and skills had been developed systematically, they were confident in expressing very creative ideas uninhibited by practical constraints. The head of department commented that 'the project exemplifies the philosophy of the course; pupils are involved in the complete process, exploring concepts and processes that impact on society' (ibid., p. 3).

By embracing the Crafts Council's 'Firing Up' initiative, designed to reinvigorate the use of kilns in schools across England, the department is working with five other schools, Wolverhampton University and Stoke University to develop more community-based ceramics projects. Although the projects are not dependent on local resources, they capitalise on historical connections to the ceramics industry so as to contextualise these broader partnership opportunities within the curriculum in an integrated way.

Systematic assessment contributes to the businesslike ethos of the department. This begins right at the start of Year 7, with an evaluation of pupils' prior experiences and skills. It is followed by continuous use of a core assessment tool that includes a focus on the personal qualities valued in the creative industries. By the sixth form, it is common for pupils to contribute each others' reviews to help support the development of core critical skills, develop an ability to reach a consensus and work as part of a team. There is frequent contact with those working in or with the creative industries, so feedback to pupils involves a wide range of views from external partners too. John Webber, a head of department at Staffordshire University, provides such feedback to pupils on a regular basis. He commented that:

> Whenever I visited the art and design department at Cheslyn Hay it feels like visiting an art school due to the dedication and professionalism of the staff, who generate tremendous enthusiasm for the subject among their pupils and their work of outstanding quality and immense breadth. As Head of Ceramics and Design at the university I led a summer school in ceramics. The Cheslyn Hay pupils worked tirelessly for six days and produced a substantial body of finished pieces. Other course leaders shared my confidence in the work ethic and foundation in the fundamentals of art and design established at the school.
>
> (Ibid., p. 5)

This case study presents a stimulating account of art, craft and design work informed by, and engaged with, a range of partners and artistic ideas drawn from the school's local community. Brickmaking and ceramic making are both substantial local industries, and the school has capitalised on this and sought to work productively with local industry to provide their pupils with a range of skills and opportunities to experience what it is actually like to be a professional artist, craftworker or designer. Within this process, there is clearly a significant element of expertise from the teachers involved. In addition to basic subject knowledge about the various arts-making practices, did you notice any of the following?

1   The teacher's commitment to contemporary and commercial practices in the arts that were part of her continuing professional development programme;
2   The broader collaborative network, facilitated by a subject association (the Crafts Council) which had drawn together six schools and two universities to share their knowledge, experience and skills in curriculum design and development;
3   The 'business' ethos within the department, which had informed assessment practices and generated meaningful processes of peer assessment as well as the input and judgements from professional artists, designers and others from the community that the pupils had learnt to really value. In fact, these were often held up by pupils who had left the school as being integral to their ability to make the transition from school into employment in these industries.

This kind of collaborative engagement with the local employers within your community will undoubtedly take time to develop. But, as this first case study illustrates, it can lead to the production of dynamic and responsive courses within curriculum areas that can help equip pupils with the skills they need for their next stage of study or even for employment within their local community.

Practical task

What are the key features of your own subject(s) that could be usefully enhanced by facilitating community links in this way? Are there local employers who you could engage with to help bring your subject to life in an alternative way? What would a partnership approach to working look like within the context of your own school?

Engagement with other schools, colleges, universities or employers is just one small part of an area-based curriculum development that seeks to work collaboratively within a local community. In Case Study 2 we will consider how such an approach can begin to raise awareness about the various groups of people that live within a local multi-faith community. It relates to the work of one primary school in Peterborough and their immediate neighbour – the Anglican Cathedral.

   This case study is drawn from the RSA's Area Based Curriculum project in Peterborough. In 2010, the RSA recruited five schools to pilot this approach. The definition of and objectives for such an approach were outlined at the end of Chapter 1 and have been restated at the beginning of this chapter. A full case study about this specific project can be found on the RSA website (RSA 2012b). What follows is an edited summary of the project drawing on this case study.

Case Study 2 Bishop Creighton and Peterborough Cathedral

Bishop Creighton Academy has around 200 pupils aged between four and eleven, and is situated within walking distance of Peterborough Cathedral. Pupils were drawn from a range of faith backgrounds. Many of the families served by the school had just arrived in Peterborough. The school had worked hard to develop a sense of agency in its pupils;

its staff were keen to build on this to develop a project that explored the role of the school and the Cathedral in the community of Peterborough. The school is physically very close to the Cathedral but in the past has made little use of it other than for Religious Education visits.

The project revolved around the production of a 'Question Time' style event in which members of the inter-faith council and of the school council sat on a panel and answered questions from the audience of Year 4 and 5 pupils. In preparation for this event, all pupils visited the Cathedral to learn about its historic place in the community. Cathedral staff visited the school and developed the debating and question-and-answer skills of pupils in preparation for the event.

The primary aim of the project was 'to develop the children's understanding of the role of the Cathedral and the school in Peterborough's wider community' (RSA 2012b, p. 4). However, this was given additional focus because during the early months of the partnership development the English Defence League, an ultra-right-wing anti-Islam group, held a march in Peterborough which had deeply affected some pupils at the school. One teacher reported that 'Some of them were really scared' (ibid.). This event strengthened the resolve of the Cathedral and the school to develop a project that allowed children of multiple faiths to explore their relationship with the wider community of Peterborough alongside the Cathedral and the inter-faith council. One teacher commented that:

> It has to be about children getting out and seeing their community – their worlds can be so small. The great thing will be for the children to meet people that they have never met before.
>
> (Ibid.)

The classes met with Cathedral officers in the autumn term and learnt about how the Cathedral came to be there and how it was built. Pupils discussed the work of the church as well as other faiths in the community and looked at what the Cathedral hoped to do.

In a skills-focused session, pupils looked at forming an idea and arguing a point. They were encouraged to develop questioning and listening skills and debating skills.

The 'Question Time' event itself was a great success, with the Bishop of Peterborough and representatives from Hindu and Catholic faiths answering children's questions about diversity and tolerance.

Both the school and the partner felt that this project was a profoundly new way of working for them. Notable differences from previous ways of working included:

- The school and the Cathedral entered into a flexible and committed partnership which allowed for a range of activities and mutual support as well as the planned project;
- The project built on existing links between the school and Cathedral to forge what both parties felt would be a permanent partnership between the two;
- Both parties benefited from the project in a genuinely joint exploration of a topic of interest to both;
- Pupils were granted a real audience and opportunity to debate matters of interest to themselves and the wider community.

The project was always about more than simply enjoyment, and teachers felt that it achieved the goals of developing children's sense of their own place in relation to Peterborough and its multi-faith community. One teacher expressed it like this:

> In terms of raising the children's awareness of themselves and where they stand in the community – that's definitely changed because they've got a much deeper understanding about where we come from and where they come from, how they connect in to the Cathedral – some of the other ... faiths that we met, and that's been really, really useful.
>
> (Ibid., p. 6)

This case study demonstrates a number of important principles that exemplify an area-based approach to curriculum development. First, it shows how the school curriculum itself can become a 'social project' that engages with the real issues facing a community, specific to time and place, through engagement with the various groups within that community and the local institutions that underpin it (in this case, the Anglican Cathedral).

During the case study, did you notice how the original objective for the curriculum was extended due to the unrest in the town caused by the English Defence League's march and the resulting effect on the young pupils? There are difficult issues to address here and the opportunity to design a responsive curriculum that challenges these issues head on would challenge many teachers. There is no doubt that in this case the school found it helpful to be working in partnership with an organisation with expertise in complex political and faith-related areas. Although there was a partnership already in existence between the school and the Cathedral, the case study demonstrates that schools often share a much broader array of concerns with community partners than perhaps both partners ever recognise! In Peterborough, it was certainly the case that the school, the Cathedral and the multi-faith community were able to draw together in a constructive way to oppose the malicious extremist views that had threatened their sense of community.

Reflective task

In light of the above case study, consider the following questions:

1   What are the recurrent social issues affecting pupils that might be addressed through the curriculum?
2   Does your school have 'natural partners' that could be drawn upon to develop learning and curriculum-related projects?
3   How might partnerships with local organisations help your school to develop a sense of identity among your pupils?

Language is central to a community. It is one of its core defining features. The next case study concerns the work of a primary school in south-east London within which around 75 per cent of pupils come from minority ethnic groups and about 60 per cent of them speak English as an additional language. We have chosen this case study as it show how crucial it is to design an area-based curriculum in conjunction with your school's local community. The full case study can be found on the Ofsted website (Ofsted 2014b). This abbreviated case study is a summary of its key points.

Case Study 3 Everyone a linguist! Learning languages at Cherry Orchard Primary School

> We have high aspirations for all our children. We believe that education is the key to every child becoming the person they need to be. Over half the children enter school with English as a second language. Every day they use this new language, English, as a vehicle for learning and social communication. To learn a modern foreign language is merely another opportunity to practise skills they already have. *We celebrate the multi-cultural society we live and learn in* and it is a natural progression to celebrate and learn about the culture of French-speaking communities across the world.
>
> (Jan Beames, Head Teacher, Cherry Orchard Primary School; emphasis added)

In the Early Years Foundation Stage, when children arrive with little English and bilingual support in their home language is unavailable, teachers at the school have developed effective strategies to settle children quickly and ensure that they acquire English as rapidly as possible. They use key greetings phrases in the children's language to make them feel at home. Contextual visual cues, expressions, music, signs and symbols are employed effectively to convey meaning. Daily contact with parents and carers encourages them to talk to their children at home in whichever is their strongest language. Pupils' language skills are steadily developed in Key Stage 1 through a lunchtime club, where they not only learn simple vocabulary, but also develop an 'ear for languages', by listening to and joining in with stories in French such as the story of 'The Very Hungry Caterpillar'.

A key strength of the curriculum is the use of well-planned cross-curricular projects. These provide a rich source of inspiring topics for French lessons and support pupils' ability to write creatively even in the early stages of their language learning. For example, the 'Voices in the Park' project created opportunities for learning verbs and how to express likes and dislikes in a meaningful and original context.

Ofsted are full of praise for the teachers who work within the school. They write:

> Teachers delivering modern language lessons have excellent subject knowledge and combine their skills as primary practitioners with a clear understanding of modern language methodology to excellent effect. Lessons are lively and great fun…. Colourful, simple 'props' are used well to bring lessons to life and encourage even the most shy to join in. Expectations are high and pupils appreciate the challenges they are given. As one pupil said, 'Lessons are really fun and challenging. When it's hard you learn more.' Technology plays its part with teachers making excellent use of interactive whiteboards and pupils' access to laptops and recording equipment such as voice boxes. Teachers make excellent use of French to manage activities in lessons. Pupils respond exceptionally well to this, because they have built up the necessary skills of inference and guessing from context, either through exposure to different languages at home, or through the constant reinforcement of these skills from the start of their time at Cherry Orchard.
>
> (Ibid., p. 2)

The French-speaking mother of a pupil at the school complimented her son's class teacher on the good work that Cherry Orchard was doing in teaching him French. She spoke of the benefits it had brought to their home life by saying, 'He has always refused to speak French at home, but since he has started learning French he has started to speak French as well as English with the family.'

As part of this excellent pedagogical approach, bilingual pupils already fluent in French are deployed as classroom assistants to support the learning of others. This helps them develop their own language skills and enhances their self-esteem.

Assessment in modern foreign languages is good and a clear system has been devised to ensure that teachers have the information they need to plan lessons that meet the needs of individual pupils very effectively. The school knows its pupils well and the linguistic skills that they bring to the school. The progress of pupils learning English as an additional language is closely tracked and monitored. As a result, they make good progress across the curriculum. The attainment of these pupils in English and mathematics at the end of Key Stage 2 in 2011 was above the average for their peers nationally and above the national average for all pupils. The pupils value their modern language portfolios that celebrate the languages that they can use; for some pupils this includes many languages.

Pupils and their families within the school and its locality speak around 25 different languages. Rather than being seen as a problem, the school regards this as a strength to be developed and particular care is taken to ensure good communications with parents and carers. The rich diversity of the community's languages is celebrated through signs and displays around the school. This includes a list on display of all the languages spoken by each year group. Pupils learning English as an additional language maintain their literacy skills in their home language(s) either through classes in 'complementary schools' (schools in the community which support the development of heritage languages) or at home with family members.

The issues associated in dealing with a multilingual community of the sort that this school serves have been engaged with in the most impressive way. This approach has been spearheaded by the senior management of the school, who have approached this as something to be celebrated rather than as an 'issue' to be dealt with. One of the key points that impressed us throughout the case study was the way that the school was proactive about forming links with their community in ways that enhanced both the educational provision within the school and the educational provision that took place outside of the school boundary. Learning outside the school was supported both in the home environment and in other non-formal educational settings. This really is 'joined-up' educational provision.

The benefits of an area-based curriculum approach for the local community have been noted in Case Studies 2 and 3. It is something that we will be returning to in the following chapters. However, it is worth mentioning here that the wider community benefits were also noted in the RSA's research. One of the principal evaluators of the project, Professor Facer, described it as the 'distribution of the educational effort' (Facer 2009, p. 3). An area-based curriculum development approach recognises that the education of young people is the concern of the community beyond the parents and the school. The establishment of a common cause between schools and local communities has been illustrated very effectively in both these case studies. These key thoughts informed the RSA's simple model for partnership working within an area-based curriculum (RSA 2012a, p. 20).

The RSA model illustrates neatly how the community partner and school objectives led to the construction of the curriculum and the various activities it contains via a consideration of the learning and wider social needs of the pupils in the school. However, the benefits or outcomes of the curriculum and its activities can impact equally on both the school and partner objectives. We like this model in that it also places the pupils at the centre of every activity while acknowledging that the benefits of curriculum development need to be felt both by schools and by their partners in order for this approach to be sustained in the longer term.

The fourth case study in this chapter comes from the work of one of this book's authors. It is drawn from a project completed during the first couple of years of the twenty-first century and concerns the relationship between a group of secondary school pupils and a group of young offenders within a nearby local prison on the east coast of Suffolk. Although these two groups of young people never met face to face, or had any direct communication, it demonstrates the power of the curriculum in facilitating knowledge, awareness and understanding of 'the other' through the artistic use of digital technologies. Following the case study itself, broader issues will be raised to conclude this chapter's focus on drawing on your local community as a source and support for area-based curriculum development.

Case Study 4 *Reflecting Others*: a digital collaboration between young people in two contrasting environments

> There are many more ways of expressing yourself rather than just talking.
>
> (Year 9 girl)

> A central challenge for the education system is to find ways of embedding learning in a range of meaningful contexts where pupils can use their knowledge and skills creatively to make an impact on the world around them.
>
> (Seltzer and Bentley 1999, p. 10)

Music lessons for pupils in Years 9 and 10 at Debenham High School were far from conventional during the Autumn 2000 and Spring 2001 terms. In them, you would have been as likely to find pupils working with digital video cameras, iMac computers, digital recorders and microphones as with traditional musical instruments. You would have found pupils recording the hustle and bustle of school life, the countryside, their hobbies and interests, and collecting audio samples from CDs and radio programmes as well as visual images from the local skateboard park and leisure centre.

In another part of Suffolk, within a highly secure special unit, young offenders were offered the opportunity to carry out a similar exercise. Both pupils and young offenders documented, through sonic and visual digital recordings, their environment and their sense of identity and community as young, twenty-first century teenagers. After the collected materials were exchanged, they become source materials for a number of sonic and visual compositions each made by one group about the other. They selected, edited and manipulated the images and sounds using a variety of innovative software tools. The sonic and visual compositions produced were arranged to make a specially designed sound and visual installation that was housed in the Exhibition Room at Snape Maltings Concert Hall. The installation was transferred to the school and the prison before returning to Snape Maltings for public viewing during that season's Aldeburgh Festival and Snape Proms.

This work, *Reflecting Others*, was an innovative digital arts project that had, at its heart, the idea of representing oneself and others through sound and image (a full analysis of the project can be found at Savage and Challis 2002). The project linked pupils in Years 9 and 10 (aged between 13 and 15 years old) with a small group of young offenders (aged between 15 and 18 years old) in the Carlford Unit at HMP Hollesley Bay. While the project involved the whole of Year 9 (approximately 84 pupils with a full range of musical ability) and took place entirely within designated music curriculum time, the prison's group of young offenders was much smaller (approximately 12) and made up of volunteers. The school pupils did have some prior experience of digital technologies within their music lessons in the *Dunwich Revisted* project that we discussed in Chapter 2 (Savage and Challis 2001); the young offenders had little or no experience of this prior to this project and worked within a designated two-hour session on a Friday afternoon. The project was organised by Aldeburgh Productions' Education Department and funded by The Monument Trust, with additional support from the J. Paul Getty Jr. Charitable Trust.

Reflecting Others used sonic and visual material collected from the pupils' and young offenders' actual environments. Three starting points (identity, community and environment) defined the process by which they selected material. The use of digital technologies was essential as a tool for gathering the material related to these responses. Pupils were able to use the minidisc player and digital video camera to collect material from any environment they chose, and subsequently to use it as source material for their pieces.

The material collected by the young offenders has fascinated pupils. This was evidenced by their rapt attention to the video artist's presentation of the video material (without sound) in the first lesson after Christmas. Pupils were very keen to ask questions about the daily routine in the life of a young offender, the offences which that they had committed (which they were not allowed to know about) and more general questions about the judicial system. The Year 10 group were equally interested in the sonic material. Seemingly insignificant things, such as the variety of young offenders' accents, were picked out by pupils as being of significant interest. The material content of some of the words and phrases used by the prisoners were commented on. Undoubtedly, some of the words and phrases that the prisoners had recorded were there for shock effect. To counterbalance this, pupils received the recording of a prisoner reading, with obvious difficulty, a poem that he had written with quiet and sombre appreciation.

The young offenders viewed the pupils as 'little rich kids'. They found their accents interesting too; they commented on how plum they sounded in comparison to theirs. The Carlford Unit is entirely male and there is no association with female prisoners. There could have been problems with female images within the male environment of the prison, and there were several comments made. The words and thoughts that the prisoners heard in the audio samples tempered these initial reactions. These turn the raw images into characters of pupils as real individuals. As the project continued we noticed a positive change in some of the prisoners' reactions to these visual materials. However, at no point during the project were pupils and young offenders able to meet, talk or contact one another.

One initially surprising thing was the similarity of responses between the two groups in certain areas. The two groups of project participants are similar ages, have ranges of similar interests and a natural curiosity for the images of the other sex. Examples of sonic and visual themes explored by both groups include:

1   Sports hall games, including basketball, badminton and squash;
2   Sounds of the cafeteria or lunch hall;
3   Weight and fitness rooms;
4   Recorded CD extracts of popular dance music.

But there are stark differences in the environment. The young offenders inhabit an internal space, with hardly any view of the outside world; the pupils were able to collect a much broader range of environmental material.

As teachers we often asked ourselves the following question: how truthful are we being in calling our project *Reflecting Others*? Were we really encouraging pupils and young offenders to give considered reflection to the 'other' within their work? It was pleasing to note in discussion with pupils that they often felt a real affinity to the young offenders through the material that they had collected. The following comment was fairly typical:

> I like it when they talked about the prison. That person described the place but it looked completely different. The 'Prisoner on the Moon' poem helped us to know what they feel like inside.
>
> (Year 10 girl)

Despite not being allowed any personal contact with the young offenders in any way, pupils did think deeply about the life of a young offender:

> By the looks of things it looks worse that I thought 'cos I expected they would be able to go outside and do more normal activities like we do. But they're trapped in there never seeing proper sunlight, trapped between walls, bars, gates and doors, trapped in Hollesley Bay for so many years and never going outside. They're looking at the same things day in, day out for years. I think this is wrong. And one boy's poem about the prison backed this up. No crime deserves to do this to a child.
>
> (Year 9 boy)

Comments like this impressed on us the value of choosing an appropriate starting point for any creative project. In providing a vehicle for pupils to challenge social agendas, for example, one is enabling them to grasp a key ingredient of artistic expression – personal communication. So often musical composition within the classroom context is divorced from pupils' life experiences as teenagers and the real value that music plays for them in expressing their identities, sense of community and environment. But authentic artistic expression is inextricably tied to life itself:

> The more we talk with children and teachers the more music becomes entangled in lives and the more its significance fades in the light of experience. The closer we look at music events in schools the more we see that music is the pretext – life is the text.
>
> (Kushner 1999, p. 216)

As project leaders and teachers, we are only too aware of the pressures that we face in fulfilling the demands of a National Curriculum. But these comments show that pupils value a chance to use a variety of artistic expressions as a way of commenting and reflecting on their lives and others.

The National Curriculum framework at the time was very different from the one that schools face today. However, it is possible to find references to curriculum development from that period that resonate with our thinking today:

> Teachers need to choose a context of relevance to young people's lives, select an interesting challenge and ensure that pupils have the necessary artistic skills. Providing choice, ensuring autonomy, encouraging teamwork, allowing experimentation and encouraging perseverance are key components of fostering creativity within the arts.
>
> (Qualification and Curriculum Authority 2000, p. 9)

The opportunity for pupils to work with a greater degree of autonomy, empowered with the tools for effective reflection on their artistic practice, was certainly an important element in the *Reflecting Others* project. Equally important was the collaborative activity within the project that was facilitated by community groups including the local prison and Aldeburgh Productions (now Aldeburgh Music; further details can be found at www.aldeburgh.co.uk). This kind of collaborative approach to the arts has a long tradition of providing 'educationally rich' experiences (Swanwick and Lawson 1999, p. 59).

In one sense, this case study brings us back to where this chapter began and the situation that most of you, as teachers, will be facing: developing an area-based curriculum approach within your own individual work. Primary school teachers may be considering how this area-based approach could helpfully project on thematic work where a range of foundation subjects are brought together; secondary school teachers may have more of a subject specialism to consider. Either way, this case study (and the first case study in this chapter) demonstrate how it is possible to build an area-based curriculum approach within your teaching that engages with your community in a productive way.

The final case studies in this chapter have a slightly different take on the notion of community and place. The philosophy behind Forest Schools is to encourage and inspire individuals of any age through positive outdoor experiences. Over recent years, many Forest School projects have been undertaken across the United Kingdom. Their key aims are to promote pupils' self-awareness, self-regulation, intrinsic motivation, empathy, independence, self-esteem, confidence, and social and communication skills. There is good evidence from a range of sources that the educational opportunities that Forest Schools provide can impact very positively on pupils' development in these areas. Further information about Forest Schools and their work can be found at their website: www.forest-schools.com.

In the following two short case studies a Forest School approach has been developed by a secondary school and a special school working in collaboration with a community partner with experience in working in this way. As you will read, in each case the school's approach was targeted on a specific group of pupils who, they felt, would benefit from this alternative form of provision.

Case Study 5a Adopting a Forest School approach with a small group of challenging Year 9 pupils

This project provided alternative educational provision for a small group of challenging Year 9 pupils from a Pupil Referral Unit (PRU) attached to a secondary school in Derbyshire. A structured three-day-per-week Forest School programme using a local woodland was developed for these pupils so as to fulfil the demands of the National Curriculum while at the same time encouraging social and emotional development. The key learning objectives of the project were for pupils to:

- Develop their relationships with peers and positive adult role models;
- Support their personal development;
- Raise self-esteem and self-confidence.

All pupils developed in a positive way, with some marked changes in behaviour being recorded both at home and in the PRU. One teacher commented that:

> Learning this way is innovative, creative and engaging. Structured activities in an outdoor woodland environment serve to remove some of the boundaries, which in the past had inhibited our disengaged youngsters from learning. As weeks went by my office slowly became full of wind chimes, hurdles, chiseled artifacts, kazoos etc. These proud pupils constantly displayed new-found confidence and skills, shared their successes for the first time, aware of their new talents but oblivious to their new-found social development.

Case Study 5b Adopting a Forest School approach for pupils at a mixed special school for pupils with severe emotional, behavioural and social difficulties

Although this project was short and involved the pupils working for only one day each week (for a term) within the forest, the teachers involved considered it successful in a number of ways for the young people involved. They were very impressed with the progress students made on individual projects and also the effort that they put into learning new skills and completing challenges.

At the beginning of the project, teachers noted that the pupils began to work mainly on solo projects and engage in solitary play. By the seventh week there were already signs of the group becoming more inclined to work and play in small groups and pairs. At the end of the project, there was very little prompting needed to encourage the pupils to help one another and most of them worked comfortably together, cooperatively with all of the other members of the group. Pupils also became a lot more conscious of the ways in which an individual's behaviour impacted on the rest of their group and would, occasionally, refuse to work with somebody else, on the basis of that person's behaviour being too disruptive for the group as a whole.

Over time, the group also became familiar with the structure of the day and the routines in place in the Forest School. This enabled them to gradually adopt the pattern of the day and meant that they felt safer and calmer in the woodland environment. At the start of the project it was a challenge to address the whole group at once and discuss the plan for the day ahead without some kind of disruption. But by the end of the project the group would sit in the log circle on arrival at the wood and ask questions about what they wanted to do that day while listening to the other planned activities. They accepted the routines and respected the reasons for having them, engaging in the whole day and planning process in a mature way.

Teachers noted a pattern in pupils' behaviour, confidence and enjoyment throughout the project. This pattern showed a period of acclimatisation at the beginning of the project consisting of fairly neutral careful behaviour. This was followed by a period of testing boundaries and experimenting with the structures after becoming more accustomed to the leaders and the site. This is nearly always followed by a period of improvement and either a return to their initial behaviour or a development and increase in appropriate behaviour beyond what was shown in the first few weeks.

All pupils progressed in terms of their interaction with others and cooperation over the course of the 14 weeks. The school expressed enthusiasm for the results they had seen and an intention to pursue further Forest School projects as a result.

We chose both parts of Case Study 5 carefully. As you have read, they relate to pupils who have either found a traditional educational approach difficult to handle, or require an alternative form of provision due to their educational needs. But it is important to state that these case studies have not been included to promote the Forest Schools' approach specifically. Rather, they are here to illustrate the important point that location, and in this case relocation, can be a powerful stimulus to new learning for an individual student and, more specifically, for groups of pupils. These two mini case studies resonate with the positive impact that an alternative location can have on pupils' attitude to learning; they remove 'boundaries to learning' that may have been built up over significant periods of time; they result in changes in patterns of behaviour and motivation; they restructure social group dynamics and allow pupils to find a new sense of common purpose.

Clearly, not everyone is going to have a forest nearby, nor the expertise needed to make maximum use of a forest if there was one helpfully positioned on the edge of your school! As we will consider further in the next chapter, the opportunities for learning in alternative spaces should be an important element in the design of an area-based curriculum. It is worth spending time thinking hard about the range of alternative learning spaces that your local community does have access to. While they might be very different to a forest, they will each present a range of opportunities that you could skilfully harness to promote a different set of learning opportunities for your pupils.

Closer to home, do not forget that every school has an outside environment of its own that you can exploit imaginatively. While it may not be as exciting as a trip to a location within the community, it would certainly prove to be less demanding in terms of your time and organisation, and less expensive to the school or parents, but could be equally rewarding. All it takes is a bit of creative thinking.

Practical task

Make a list of possible locations within your local community where you could relocate a class, or small group of pupils, for a short period of time. Alternatively, how can you exploit your school environment to help develop alternative learning opportunities in an imaginative way?

For either case, think through the possible benefits of making a more explicit use of an alternative location in terms of pupils' educational development. Are any of the benefits that you have read about in Case Study 5 achievable within your school environment or a local community setting?

Moving forward: the principles and purposes of an area-based approach to curriculum development

The end of this chapter marks the mid-point of our book. In the chapters that follow, we will be moving forward our discussion about an area-based approach to curriculum development in a number of new directions: in relation to the formation of your pedagogy (in Chapter 6), in respect of the challenges of the digital age and how that redefines what is meant by 'local' (in Chapter 7), and through a more detailed examination of partnership approaches (in Chapter 8). Our book will conclude with a chapter that will help you evaluate any specific pieces of curriculum development that you want to undertake in your own teaching.

Throughout this book we have adopted our key definition for an area-based curriculum from the substantial body of work being undertaken by the RSA. This definition has been presented at the beginning of Chapters 2, 3, 4 and 5 as we have considered the various themes or characteristics of our locations that we can draw on to construct an area-based curriculum.

Each of the previous four chapters has also presented a series of case studies that have explore various aspects of this definition through the work of innovative teachers across the breadth of the United Kingdom and from a range of different types of schools.

At the end of Chapter 2, we drew a parallel between an area-based curriculum development process and a cross-curricular approach to teaching and learning. A cross-curricular approach was defined as being 'characterised by sensitivity towards, and a synthesis of, knowledge, skills and understandings from various subject areas; these inform an enriched pedagogy that promotes an approach to learning which embraces and explores this wider sensitivity through various methods (Savage 2011, pp. 8–9).

There are two sets of key words in this definition that are worthy of highlighting.

First, notice the three 'S' words: sensitivity, synthesis and subject. These refer to the ways in which you should approach the knowledge, skills and understanding inherent within every curriculum subject. These are exemplified in curriculum documents but also have a historical legacy that is underpinned in various ways, not least in teachers' and others' conceptions about a particular subject and how it should be taught. Understanding this is a vital step that needs to be taken before moving into collaborative curriculum ventures.

These 'S' words refer equally to the act of teaching. In other words, they are important, informing teaching principles that impact on learning. Neither an area-based curriculum development approach nor a cross-curricular pedagogy is about weakening or watering-down subjects in any way. Rather, they are about the development of an enhanced curriculum pedagogy that a skilful teacher adopts for the explicit purposes of enhancing teaching and learning. This leads on to the second set of important key words, the 'E' words: enriching, embracing and exploring.

A new, enriched area-based curriculum, underpinned by a cross-curricular pedagogy, will embrace and explore your sensitivity towards, and synthesis of, the different knowledge, skills and understanding within curriculum subjects. In order for this to happen, there are at least two premises: first, you will need to embrace an understanding of your locality in terms of its geography, its history, its culture and its sense of community (this is what the previous four chapters have been about!); second, you will need to ensure that your subject knowledge is extended beyond your own subject area in order to make the right and productive links to that local context. When this occurs, you will be in a position to develop an area-based curriculum approach that utilises a range of methods in line with the following principles and purposes.

The principles of area-based curriculum development

Area-based curriculum development is:

- Based on individual subjects and their connections through authentic links at the level of curriculum content, key concept or learning process, or through an external theme/dimension;

- Characterised and developed by individual teachers with excellent subject knowledge, a deep understanding of their subject culture and a capacity to reconceptualise this within a broader context of learning beyond the subject and school boundary, and with sensitivity towards other subject cultures;
- As much about a the development of a skilful pedagogy as anything else;
- Coherent in its maintaining of links with pupils' prior learning and experience;
- Contextualised effectively, presenting opportunities for explicit links with pupils' learning outside the formal classroom in a range of settings including the home and local community;
- Demanding in its use of curriculum time and resources, requiring flexibility and often needing the support of senior managers if it is to be implemented effectively;
- Underpinned by a meaningful assessment process that is explicitly linked to, and informed by, the enriched pedagogical framework;
- Normally collaborative in its nature, requiring meaningful and sustained cooperation between teachers with support from senior managers.

The purposes of area-based curriculum development

The purposes of area-based curriculum development flow from an understanding of the RSA definition and our principles described above. As with the principles, these purposes benefit teachers and pupils alike.

The purposes of area-based curriculum development are to:

- Motivate and encourage pupils' learning in a sympathetic way in conjunction with their wider life experiences as 'bounded' by their local community;
- Draw on similarities in and between individual subjects and their exemplification in wider life (in terms of subject content, pedagogical devices and learning processes) and make these links explicit in various ways;
- Provide active and experiential learning for pupils within a broad range of settings within their community;
- Develop meaningful cooperation and collaboration between school staff and community partners leading to a range of mutual benefits;
- Promote pupils' cognitive, personal and social development in an integrated way through the use of a range of learning contexts inside and outside the school;
- Allow teachers the opportunity to evaluate and reflect on their teaching and to be imaginative and innovative in their curriculum planning;
- Facilitate a shared vision among teachers, managers, community leaders, local employers, parents and others through meaningful collaborations at all levels of curriculum development and design.

The first five chapters of this book have sought to establish and illustrate the benefits of area-based curriculum and an accompanying pedagogy. In line with the key principles outlined in Chapter 1, it has placed the individual teacher at the heart of this particular innovation. The teacher takes a core role as an initiator of curricular design and reform. We have sought to understand this potentially innovative approach from the teacher outwards, rather than invest the teacher with external meanings and priorities. We hope that this had led to you feeling some kind of empowerment! Through this process, it is hoped that some of the peculiarities of individual subjects and associated pedagogies can be understood, acknowledged and, on occasions, moved aside in the pursuit and production of an enriched, area-based curriculum development and associated pedagogy.

References

DfE (Department for Education) (2014) *National Curriculum in England: Framework for key stages 1 to 4*. www.gov.uk/government/publications/national-curriculum-in-england-framework-for-key-stages-1-to-4/the-national-curriculum-in-england-framework-for-key-stages-1-to-4 [last accessed 31 March 2014].

Facer, K. (2009) 'Towards an Area Based Curriculum? Creating space for the city in schools'. *International Journal of Educational Research*, 55, pp. 16–25.

Forest Schools (2014) *Case Study: How a secondary school can implement Forest Schools into their setting*. www.forestschools.com/case-studies/secondary-school [last accessed 1 April 2014].

Kushner, S. (1999) 'Fringe Benefits: Music education out of the National Curriculum'. *Music Education Research* 1:2, pp. 209–218.

Ofsted (Office for Standards in Education, Children's Services and Skills) (2014a) www.ofsted.gov.uk/resources/goodpractice [last accessed 24 March 2014].

Ofsted (2014b) 'Good Practice Resource: Making art, craft and design education relevant to life and work: Cheslyn Hay Sport and Community High School'. www.ofsted.gov.uk/resources/good-practice-resource-making-art-craft-and-design-education-relevant-life-and-work-cheslyn-hay-spor [last accessed 28 March 2014].

Ofsted (2014c) 'Good Practice Resource: Everyone a linguist: Cherry Orchard Primary School'. www.ofsted.gov.uk/resources/good-practice-resource-everyone-linguist-cherry-orchard-primary-school [last accessed 24 March 2014].

QCA (Qualifications and Curriculum Authority) (2000) *The Arts, Creativity and Cultural Education: An international perspective*. London, QCA.

RSA (Royal Society for the encouragement of Arts, Manufactures and Commerce) (2012a) *Thinking About an Area-based Curriculum: A guide for practitioners*. London, RSA. www.thersa.org/__data/assets/pdf_file/0016/1000771/RSA_Thinking-About-an-Area-based-Curriculum-A-Guide-for-Practitioners.pdf [last accessed 3 February 2015].

RSA (2012b) *Bishop Creighton Academy and Peterborough Cathedral: Peterborough curriculum case study*. www.thersa.org/action-research-centre/learning,-cognition-and-creativity/education/practical-projects/area-based-curriculum/reports-and-case-studies/peterborough-curriculum-case-study-bishop-creighton-academy-and-peterborough-cathedral [last accessed 24 March 2014].

Savage, J. (2011) *Cross-Curricular Teaching and Learning in the Secondary School*. London, Routledge.

Savage, J. and Challis, M. (2001) 'Dunwich Revisited: Collaborative composition and performance with new technologies'. *British Journal of Music Education* 18:2, pp. 139–149.

Savage, J. and Challis, M. (2002) 'A Digital Arts Curriculum? Practical ways forward'. *Music Education Research* 4:1, pp. 7–24.

Seltzer, K. and Bentley, T. (1999) 'The Creative Age: Knowledge and skills for the new economy'. London, DEMOS.

Swanwick, K. and Lawson, D. (1999) 'Authentic Music and its Effect on the Attitudes and Musical Development of Secondary School Pupils'. *Music Education Research* 1:1, pp. 47–60.

Chapter 6

Devising an area-based curriculum and a cross-curricular pedagogy

> It is schooling that has reduced knowledge to 'subjects' and teaching to mere telling.
> (Alexander 2008, p. 141)

Introduction

This chapter will explore how an active engagement with geographical, historical cultural and societal understanding of place, as we have discussed in the previous four chapters, can be helpfully developed through area-based curriculum and an associated pedagogy. Within the primary school, this pedagogical approach might be suitable for thematic or project work; within the secondary school, this approach will helpful to the teaching of any subject. In both contexts, this approach could usefully inform ways of working in partnership with other groups outside of the traditional school setting. This chapter will focus on how individual teachers can develop their own pedagogy through a broad approach to an area-based curriculum process that explores their locality and makes connections to it in meaningful ways. Before addressing this directly, our chapter will begin by exploring three key areas in curriculum development, namely your pedagogy, your pupils and your subject. We will then move on to consider some of the specific issues related to the construction of an area-based curriculum approach within your teaching.

Understanding pedagogy

If our schools are going to facilitate an educational process that is more than teachers 'telling' pupils about individual 'subjects' (Alexander 2008, p. 141), our argument here is that there needs to be a major change in the type of pedagogy that every teacher, regardless of their subject or the phase of education within which they are working, should seek to fully understand and adopt. For us, pedagogy is more than just a way of acting as a teacher. It involves a way of thinking and a way of knowing; it exists within a relationship of people, resources and ideas. Many of these aspects of a pedagogy will be grounded within your locality and need to be understood, appreciated and engaged with if your teaching is to make a positive impact within, and make connections to, your local context.

One of the most influential figures in recent discussions surrounding pedagogy has been Robin Alexander. As a Fellow of Wolfson College at the University of Cambridge and Director of the Cambridge Primary Review, his influence of educational policy has been significant in recent years. Alexander defines pedagogy as:

The act of teaching together with its attendant discourse. It is what one needs to know, and the skills one needs to command, in order to make and justify the many different kinds of decisions of which teaching is constituted.

(Alexander 2004, p. 11)

Alexander reinforces our key point that pedagogy is not the same as teaching. Pedagogy involves teaching, but it also includes an 'attendant discourse' that comprises knowledge and skills. These inform and justify decision-making processes within teaching. In particular, Alexander's two conceptions of 'pedagogy as discourse' and 'pedagogy as act' are worthy of contemplation. We will be using these ideas throughout this chapter at various points to frame our discussion about the development of an area-based approach to curriculum development.

Pedagogy as discourse is conceived around three interrelated levels of ideas that relate to the classroom, the system (including policies that determine the system) and wider aspects of society and culture. All of these, Alexander asserts, 'enable, formalise and locate the act of teaching' (ibid.). All of them also reinforce the central point of our argument here: your pedagogy is implicitly mediated by your locality. We will illustrate this in a number of different ways.

First, for the classroom, Alexander lists four key attributes or ideas that you will need to consider in order to develop an effective pedagogy:

- Pupils: their characteristics, development, motivation, needs and differences;
- Learning: nature, facilitation, achievement, assessment;
- Teaching: nature, scope, planning, execution, evaluation;
- Curriculum: ways of knowing, doing, creating, investigating, making sense.

The first of these attributes is the most important for our discussion here. Understanding your pupils, how their personalities have developed, their wider lives and the formative influences that have characterised their lives are all vital starting points for your pedagogy. To put it more bluntly, teaching pupils in inner-city Leeds will not be the same as teachings pupils in rural Cornwall. It is vital that you contextualise your pedagogy, in this general sense, within your school's locality. To do otherwise would be to create a dissonance with your pupils' broader lives and experiences within that locality.

Second, Alexander identifies the 'system' or 'policy' level as an important formalising and legitimising frame for your pedagogy. Again, there are four main attributes to consider:

- School: infrastructure, staffing, training;
- Curriculum: aims, content;
- Assessment: formal tests, qualifications, entry requirements;
- Other policies: teacher recruitment and training, equity and inclusion.

While we could discuss each of these in some length, perhaps it is the first of them, the school, that is worthy of an additional comment here. As we have discussed throughout our book, the school, its physical buildings, its staff and pupils all exist within a locality. The geography, history, culture and sense of community within that locality will all influence the way that the school operates (its infrastructure), the key decision-making processes within the school (as these are carried out by governors, senior leaders and staff within these school, all of whom will normally be part of that locality) and the attitudes, opinions, skills and understanding of staff at the school who, to a greater or lesser extent, will be drawn from that locality too. It is important to remember that this influence also works the other way around. A school can be a very powerful influence on the locality within which it is placed, either for good or for ill.

Alexander's third level of pedagogical discourse relates to our culture and society. These ideas, he suggests, locate our teaching very explicitly and it is perhaps here, even more than the previous two points, that the ideas of an area-based curriculum will find most resonance. Alexander highlights the following three key attributes:

- Community: the familial and local attitudes, expectations and mores that shape learners' outlooks;
- Culture: the collective ideas, values, customs and relationships that shape a society's view of itself, of the world and of education;
- Self: what it is to be a person; how identity is acquired.

While you could read the point about 'culture' as relating to a national context (and that would certainly be true), we think that it is also the case that all three of these key points play an important part within the local context too. We explored this at length in Chapter 4. The sense of community that exists within your locality relates directly to your school, and your school plays an important part in shaping that in return. The cultural identity of your locality and that of your school are equally powerful and intrinsically linked. The notion of individual identity and how this is formed is contextualised within a local community and culture. This final point is so important that we are going to explore it further using a slightly different set of ideas. These relate to the second key foundational point that we want to emphasis in relation to our opening theme of curriculum development.

Reflective task

Take each of Alexander's three points in turn and reflect on how they are represented within your own teaching at your school. Are there any additional dimensions within your pedagogy that are relevant to our chapter's theme?

Understanding your pupils and your role in curriculum development

> One of the artifices of evaluation is to portray individuals but to invest them (and their lives) with meanings derived from the projects in which we observe them – like clothing dolls. ... Instead of drawing a boundary around a project experience and reading individual lives within the context of the project, we need, just a little more often, to consider life experiences as contexts within which to understand educational projects.
>
> (Kushner 1993, p. 39)

Saville Kushner is one of the world's leading experts on educational evaluation. Over the years, he has worked on a range of projects exploring the nature of evaluation, how it can be done well and how participants within projects, as well as those observing them, can benefit from adopting a rich evaluative perspective. In Chapter 9 we will be drawing further on his work as we consider how to effectively evaluate a piece of area-based curriculum development.

In the above quotation, Kushner's argument is that evaluation is often done in a way that ignores the most crucial issue, namely the importance of gaining insights about a particular project from the rich context of an individual's experience of life. To make this point explicit for our discussion on pedagogy and an area-based curriculum, we could illustrate this by adapting it to describe the relationship between schools and their pupils:

> One of the artifices of *curriculum development* is to *consider pupils and their needs* but to *make assumptions about what is important for them* derived from the *curriculum frameworks that we consider important* – like clothing dolls. Instead of drawing a boundary around a *unit of work* and reading individual lives within the context of *that unit*, we need, just a little more often, to consider life experiences as contexts within which to understand *and situate curriculum development*.
>
> (After Kushner 1993, p. 39)

If we start with the notion of wanting to write and teach a unit of work based on an area-based curriculum approach, and seek to understand and develop this in isolation from the people involved in that locality, investing meaning and applying principles without respect to their wider experiences contained within that area, we will produce something of only very limited value in terms of promoting meaningful and sustained educational engagement. Much better, Kushner suggests, is to face up to the challenge to start with and commit to developing a rich understanding of your locality and all its various features, individuals and associated life stories. Having done this, use this understanding as the context from within which to develop a process of curriculum development and the construction of curriculum materials and, ultimately, to infuse this understanding into your pedagogy.

Kushner's comments challenge contemporary thinking about curriculum reform and development that are often remote to the lives of teachers, dictated through national policies with little consideration given to local contexts. But, as we have explored at various points throughout our book, the changes in the National Curriculum and school autonomy have given you a real (and legitimate) opportunity to pursue alternative approaches within your school.

Reflective task

- How do my perceptions of my locality affect my choice of pedagogy and the opportunities for learning that I present to my pupils?
- How have my wider life experiences shaped my identity as a teacher within this local community?
- How can I gain a greater understanding of my pupils' life experiences?

Kushner's challenge to us is to seek, first and foremost, to understand curriculum development through the context of one's own life experience. How can we do this in a constructive way?

Peshkin's work on subjectivity provides us with one approach that we could adopt. Defining 'subjectivity' as 'the quality of an investigator that affects the results of observational investigation' (Peshkin 1988, p. 17), he highlights the requirement for teachers to be 'meaningfully attentive' (ibid.) to their own subjectivity as they conduct and reflect on their teaching activities. Peshkin describes subjectivity as a 'garment that cannot be removed' which has the capability to 'filter, skew, shape, block, transform, construe, and misconstrue what transpires' during any given sequence of thought or action (ibid.). Perhaps Peshkin's greatest exemplification of this idea was extended piece of research at Riverview High School in California where he investigated issues of racial identity, segregation and ethnicity. You can read more about this study in his book *The Color of Strangers, the Color of Friends* (Peshkin 1991).

There are number of important points here. First, Peshkin established the concept of a 'subjective I'. These are the highly individual and personal attitudes or ways of thinking that colour our subjectivity. The foundations for Peshkin's own subjective I's were drawn from a range of sources, including:

- His own belief and value systems;
- His experiences of a particular environment, i.e. the town of 'Riverview';
- His ongoing experiences of life within the particular school;
- The wider community and the relationships that he, and other members of his family, established within that community.

Did you notice how many of these relate directly to the local area of Riverview? (The right answer is three out of four.) This was so important to Peshkin that he moved himself and his family to live within the Riverview community for several years while he conducted his research project. He felt that it was impossible to understand the processes of education within that school, and how they impacted on the issues of race and ethnicity, without him and his family being part of that local community for themselves.

Peshkin categorises subjective I's in two main ways:

- 'Intrinsic Subjectivities' that make up our whole reflective 'being', i.e. they are contextless and are born out of genetic disposition and early formative years;
- 'Situational Subjectivities' that change from place to place, i.e. they are contextualised in some way.

Practical task 1

Can you analyse your own intrinsic I's? You could try to do this in a number of ways, but it is a highly personal exercise. Reflect on the key notions or concepts that underpin your beliefs about teaching and learning. Other processes of thought can help you define and refine your chosen intrinsic I's. Think through:

- Underpinning beliefs or philosophies (beyond the educational) about your subject and the impact it has had on your life throughout your childhood and formative years;
- Your own educational experiences and memories through formal and informal contexts (i.e. school, university, but also the home, local community, etc.);

- Conversations (or recollections of conversations) with key people that you have met who may have changed the way you think or feel about your subject;
- Your reading and the powerful ideas that this may have contained which may have impacted you personally or educationally;
- Family or other relationships and how these may have shaped your personality and affected your teaching ability;
- 'Eureka' moments from your own life experiences that have shaped your personality.

There will undoubtedly be all kinds of other sources for your ideas here too.

Labelling your intrinsic I's is difficult but important. Try to get down to the base level here and ensure that each 'I' has a distinctive 'flavour' or 'personality'. Putting ideas into categories can help with this process. Try and end up with four or five intrinsic I's of your own. This will help you in the next stage of the exercise later in this chapter.

For Peshkin, intrinsic I's are the dominant voices in how we perceive our work as a teacher. Our intrinsic I's come into play at key moments of innovation or change within our personal or professional lives. For our purposes here, this could relate closely to the development of a new area-based approach to curriculum development.

Understanding the academic subject in curriculum development

> School subject communities are neither harmonious nor homogeneous and members do not necessarily share particular values, subject definitions and interests.
>
> (Jephcote and Davies 2007, p. 210)

Peshkin's concept of intrinsic I's provides a lens through which one can generate a more holistic view of oneself, one's beliefs and core values and how they might impact on one's teaching. Understanding oneself is an important prerequisite for meaningful collaboration with others.

But there is a third vital set of connections that you will need to understand fully in relation to curriculum development before developing an area-based curriculum and pedagogy. These connections concern one of the most important building-blocks of nearly every school's curriculum: academic subjects.

All teachers, whether teaching in a primary or secondary school, work within a subject-based culture that is underpinned by significant historical legacies. These can lead to fundamental differences of opinion about what should be taught within a particular subject and how it should be taught and assessed. Jephcote and Davies give a flavour of the complexity of the situation through their notion of the 'teacher as actor'; someone who has to work within three different contexts or levels (the micro, meso and macro) in order to present the subject as a meaningful 'whole' within the curriculum:

> Changing the curriculum is an outcome of contexts between actors in different arenas and at different levels. Its story needs to be told at a number of levels to

reflect the membership and structure of subject communities and to provide a means of illustrating each level and their interconnectedness. At the micro-level accounts have been concerned mainly with teachers, school classrooms and subjects and at macro-level with processes of policy-making and its implementation. At the same time, the meso-level has been taken to comprise of subject associations, local education authorities and sponsored curriculum projects where there are mediating processes which provide means to reinterpret macro-level changes and to assess the range of new choices they present to subject factions.

(Jephcote and Davies 2007, p. 208)

Clearly, the assumption that school subjects are harmonious and homogeneous in their relationships with one another is false. Subjects may have a range of competing values, definitions and interests that can lead to conflict and tension, both within and across subjects. Goodson and Mangen's concept of a 'subject culture' (Goodson and Mangen 1998, p. 120) is instructive here. For them, subject cultures are the 'identifiable structures which are visibly expressed through classroom organisation and pedagogical styles'. They are what makes a particular subject unique and, in a simple sense, are what portray to pupils the sense that they are studying a particular subject at a specific moment in the school day.

Reflective task

What is your specialist subject? How would you define the subject culture that relates to this? How does this culture relate to other subjects within your school?

Developing an area-based curriculum approach in your teaching

An appreciation of Peshkin's concept of the intrinsic I allows you to move from a position of strength and security within yourself, and your pedagogy, to form connections with other subjects and sets of ideas or develop collaborations with other people and groups across your locality. As we have seen, appreciating that academic subjects are different and embed a range of pedagogical approaches and techniques is also essential as you seek to broaden out your understanding of curriculum development into a local, area-based approach.

Alongside Peshkin and Robin Alexander, the work of Lawrence Stenhouse has featured strongly in this book. As you will remember, he became famous for his adage that there is no curriculum development without teacher development. We are mindful of one particular question that he posed that relates directly to our key point that curriculum development must also be directly linked to one's locality and the life experiences of pupils within that particular area:

The problem of the curriculum can now be expressed as follows: what worthwhile curriculum content can we find as a focus for a classroom experience which will stimulate the pupils to an attempt to find for themselves standards which are worthwhile and viable in terms of their own experience of life?

(Stenhouse 1975, p. 133)

Stenhouse's question challenges head on the conception of the curriculum as a closed network of content managed and controlled by a teacher or an examination board. These, by default, are the exact opposite of what Stenhouse believed was needed in schools. Predetermined outcomes to perceived educational deficiencies within pupils, however helpfully presented by a teacher, are second-rate when compared to Stenhouse's vision of classrooms as 'cultural laboratories' within which these relationships between school and community could be explored:

> The classroom becomes a kind of cultural laboratory in which new face-to-face culture is generated at a humble level. The pupils are in fact not making a transition from one culture to another, but rather being provided with the opportunity to feed their own culture on the arts and sciences, and thus to build for themselves an enriched medium of communication and thinking. ... The teacher ought to be a servant of his [sic] pupils, asking himself how his subject can make a contribution to the quality of their living.
>
> (Stenhouse 1975, p. 134)

Stenhouse's vision is that curriculum development of the type that we have been discussing in this chapter can become a powerful agent of change for pupils both in and, very importantly, beyond school. While we should always recognise and promote the importance of using our locality for curriculum development, we should also be strong advocates for the transformative power that educational opportunities and experiences can have in the lives of our young people. After all, is not that why you came into teaching?

Practical task 2

Review your notes from Practical task 1. Imagine that you have been asked to produce a short unit of work that explores a specific aspect of your local area, to be taught within the normal timetabled arrangements at your school. You have agreed a focus for the unit of work and are at the point of putting a few preliminary ideas together. This is a new 'situation' that you find yourself in. It will challenge your 'intrinsic I's' in new ways.

Consider the following questions:

1   What advantages or possibilities are there within the incorporation of the area-based context of your new unit of work? How can you maximise these within the unit of work that you are planning?
2   Are there any disadvantages that you can anticipate arising from the proposed unit and its area-based approach? Which boundaries will be difficult to cross? Why?
3   What key principles or ideas within your subject, and the way that you have conceived this individually or culturally within your school, will be affected by this new area-based approach? Will there be comprises to be made?
4   What key principles or ideas from the intrinsic I's that you identified in Practical task 1 can be developed throughout this unit of work? How can your intrinsic I's become situational I's that can usefully empower your pedagogy as you deliver this unit of work?
5   What, if any, new partnerships will you need to form to put together a meaningful and coherent unit of work that addresses your chosen theme?

Developing an area-based curriculum

Throughout this book, we have drawn on some of the key ideas and approaches adopted by and developed within the RSA's Area Based Curriculum project. Their responses to some of the questions contained within Practical task 2 are outlined in their four 'ideal types' of area-based curriculum (RSA 2012a, p. 14). These four types of area-based curriculum are not mutually exclusive. In reality, bits of several approaches are likely to characterise your own process of curriculum development. But they do present an interesting set of options that you could consider as you begin the process of designing an area-based curriculum for yourself

1   Add-on local curriculum:
   • Separate timetable or 'subject' for local curriculum;
   • Curriculum 'about' a place regardless of relevance to traditional subject knowledge;
   • Attempt to reflect and involve local families, communities and realities, including immediate environs of school.
2   Locally enhanced curriculum:
   • Local area examples drawn upon throughout subject teaching;
   • Links made with traditional subjects but mainstream knowledge not challenged;
   • Local 'experts' and high-status resources drawn upon to support mainstream curriculum.
3   Co-constructed curriculum:
   • Local stakeholders and schools talk about educational purpose and design curriculum together;
   • Local stakeholders feel 'ownership' over the learning of pupils in school;
   • School curriculum is a 'social project' oriented to serve the purposes of the pupils and their community.
4   School-led local curriculum:
   • Schools decide upon a non-traditional curriculum model which allows for local links;
   • What is important/relevant about the locality is decided upon and linked to by the school;
   • Local 'experts' and high-status resources drawn upon to support curriculum model.

(Ibid.)

We are not suggesting that any one of these approaches is more ideal or appropriate than any other. Neither are they presented in any order of priority. Rather, it would be a useful activity to use these statements to consider the nature of the curriculum that you are seeking to develop, what you might need to change to get there, who would agree with your position (or disagree), and to what extent each of the curriculum types would be 'about', 'by' or 'for' a place.

The curriculum models offered by the RSA are also differentiated by the ways in which you might perceive the curriculum to be fixed or flexible and also by how you would characterise the relationship between the school curriculum and the local area. Key questions that you could ask yourself would include:

* Is the local area there to support the mainstream school curriculum?
* Does the school curriculum have a legitimate role to play in transforming the local area?
* Who should decide what is important or not within any given curriculum model?

The answers to these questions will all help unveil a range of different viewpoints that relate closely to our own intrinsic dispositions on what is important and valuable about the educational process. Be prepared for a debate if you share these with your colleagues both within your school and in your local community.

This point about community and partnership working leads us on to the first of four key points about developing an area-based curriculum approach in your teaching.

I Developing an area-based curriculum approach in your teaching: making partnerships central to your work

The RSA's Area Based Curriculum that we have been discussing in the previous section was based on two key ideas:

* It uses the locality to illustrate the content of the National Curriculum, making the latter more relevant and engaging to young people, and increasing their sense of identity with, and understanding of, the local area;
* It is owned and created locally, by multiple stakeholders working with schools (including for example parents, pupils, local businesses and organisations, community groups and so on).

The project aspired to challenge the dominant view of a top-down, hierarchical curriculum based on a limited range of high-status knowledge. Having read the vast amount of educational literature produced by the project, we are happy to subscribe to the view that this was certainly the case. The project did support schools and their local communities in a process of imagining what an area-based curriculum should look like. It also evaluated the impact of this and drew together some useful lessons for us (which we will consider later in this chapter).

The project as a whole explored in considerable detail the ways in which school-based partnerships can help promote an area-based curriculum. However, this was seldom easy. In her case study report of the Manchester-based case studies, the project evaluator Professor Keri Facer reported that the schools' attempts to partner with external organisations were often subject to significant frustrations including:

* Teachers' lack of time and support for administration and networking;
* Lack of clear contacts in external organisations;
* No shared or central point for sharing contacts with external partners;
* The logistical challenges of transporting hundreds of children to different locations, including the associated demands for risk assessment, staff support and transport costs;

- The costs of visiting external organisations. Schools adopted different approaches to building external links: some were confident enough to ask for access and resources at no cost, others were less confident and paid for all activities.

(RSA 2009, p. 2)

Even when schools did take risks and sought to develop true partnerships within which to develop their area-based curriculum (rather than simply commissioning an external organisation to write the curriculum for them – which, incidentally, we think is always a very bad idea), a number of other problems tended to follow fairly rapidly:

> Their surprise at this [being welcomed as a potential partner for a potential collaboration] meant that they often did not brief organisations well enough in advance or work carefully with them to develop activities, often for fear of seeming ungrateful. Teachers' concerns to develop curriculum and activities that could be repeated in subsequent years also meant that many were concerned about possible risks of working with external partners on a collaborative basis in case this meant that they would have to develop new partners in subsequent years. This, combined with the typically fluid processes of curriculum design, meant that schools didn't work with partners to design curriculum and instead tended to build a partnership characterised by 'commissioning' or 'visiting' arrangements – buying-in expertise or finding locations to visit.

(Ibid.)

Clearly, partnership working of this type is not easy. Curriculum development, even when based on a theme related to a specific locality, is not easily shared.

The RSA's work in Peterborough does seem to us to have been significantly more successful than its work in Manchester. Lessons from the four Manchester case studies (RSA 2009) were acted upon and the work in Peterborough, as written by Louise Thomas (RSA 2012b), present a genuinely interesting account of productive partnership working and community engagement. In addition to the basic three-part definition that the RSA adopted for the project as a whole (which we explored at the end of Chapter 1), within the work at Peterborough the five schools that the RSA worked with were each required to design a project that:

- Connected with a part of the curriculum of schools;
- Was designed by schools in collaboration with local community partners;
- Was supported by local expertise and context;
- Was taught using the local area as a classroom; and
- Contained objectives both for young people and for community partners.

(RSA 2012b, p. 9)

The perceived benefits for pupils, schools and community partners in this form of partnership working were described as being as follows:

- Access to local expertise and resources to support learning;
- Access to sites for learning in the locality that could be used;
- Alternative perspectives on learning, education, and the locality;

- Learning about, by and for Peterborough;
- Shared ownership of the learning going on in schools, providing common cause between schools and other local stakeholders;
- A range of sustainable relationships between schools and local stakeholders which could be drawn upon in different ways;
- Direct, positive contact for pupils with adults from a range of sectors and backgrounds.

(Ibid., p. 22)

The report presents a series of lively reflections on these aspirations from the voices of key members of staff, pupils and community participants. They make for encouraging reading. We present a few below to give you a flavour of the key benefits that they felt in relation to this approach:

Teacher, Junior School

I ... thought ... it would be dead hard to engage with ... I thought ... 'Crikey, it's going to be really hard to develop a relationship with someone to a point where you can collaborate for joint goals' ... I thought that it sounded quite difficult. Um, and then ... it wasn't!

Peterborough Cathedral Schools and Community Officer

Some days it was just me talking with them about their curriculum. ... It was very little to do with visiting or involving the Cathedral – the Cathedral's role was providing me as a kind of support. And I think that was entirely appropriate – we had that connection and as I say that's one of the things it throws up – you have somebody else there, another resource, someone else to throw ideas in.

Deputy Head, Primary School

We already knew ... bringing people in would add ... another layer to what you're already doing – more specialist knowledge ... it changes the way you look at the learning, so that you don't become too narrow with your perspective.

Year 5 student

I learnt like, what can be done if you get like a good team together and help – because that's what [the partner organisation] did with their nature reserve ... I learnt that sometimes if something doesn't go well, like with [the partner], just by doing a little bit each day you can make something really good.

Year 8 student

If you, like, live here ... you're like 'aw, I just live in Peterborough', but you could be like, 'aw, I live in Peterborough, do you know John Clare came here' because he was a good poet.

So, even within the auspices of the same project, we can see that partnership working with the local community around your school can be problematic but, simultaneously, very beneficial! It will certainly be hard work and will require a significant amount of time. For this reason, it is probably best facilitated by a whole-school approach rather than you, as an individual member of staff, having to shoulder all the work and responsibilities yourself. With this in mind, what are the keys to effective partnership working of this type?

i Putting the pupils first

Most importantly, all partners, whether they are local employers, external voluntary agencies or other educational institutions, must share the responsibility for the care and welfare needs of the pupils and must put in support to ensure that these needs are catered for. This goes far beyond issues of safety in alternative learning environments (which we will consider below). It is about a shared and common understanding of safeguarding and child protection. Although we are emphasising here that this is a shared concern, the reality is that it will be your school's responsibility to ensure that appropriate arrangements are put in place when working in partnership with other groups.

ii Ensure that area-based curriculum development with partners is explicitly linked to broader curriculum frameworks

This is a tricky issue. One of the key challenges that the RSA found in relation to their work in Peterborough was that some schools (and this was mainly found to be secondary schools) could not create a coherent link between an area-based curriculum of the type we are promoting here and the traditional curriculum that led to standardised assessments (e.g. at the end of Key Stage 3 or via national examination frameworks). It seemed that the root of this problem lay in schools considering an area-based curriculum development as being 'separate from' and often 'in competition with' work done in a traditional classroom (RSA 2012b, p. 35).

This was highlighted in many of the comments made by teachers and evaluators within the project. For example, here is one teacher at secondary school:

> I think we're at a crossroads. It has resonated with lots of members of staff, but I think that it still remains to be seen ... given the demands the government are putting upon us with these other more what you could argue more engaging, wholesome or holistic approaches to teaching and learning, I think we've got some big decisions to make on that front.
>
> (RSA 2012b, p. 36)

This point was picked up within the project evaluation:

> The RSA found difficulty in developing conversations in secondary schools about how area-based activities could make a positive contribution to the quality of subject learning and to examination attainments, and some offers of help in this direction were not taken up. This suggests that the 'performance

orientation' mentioned earlier in this report has found an affinity with a narrow view of subject teaching.

(Ibid.)

These observations emphasise to us the importance of ensuring that significant thought is given by the school to how new forms of curriculum development of the type we are promoting in this book are related closely to the key assessment outcomes and performance indicators by which schools are monitored and judged. However, we would also want to state very clearly that these ideas are not in opposition to each other. We believe that is perfectly possible to have a healthy, innovative and creative process of curriculum development at play within a school, one that draws in and works constructively with a range of partners, while still performing well against traditional measurements of success.

This point was also noted in the RSA's evaluation of their work in Peterborough. During the project, one primary school had its Ofsted grade downgraded from 'good' to 'satisfactory'. Rather than withdraw from the project, the head teacher maintained the links with the RSA and the school's commitment to developing an area-based curriculum with its partners. The result was beneficial both in terms of the project itself and the school's wider commitment to improve. The evaluator noted that:

> Importantly, the process of enhancing learning through the initiative was seen by the key teachers involved as either superior to (and a prior condition for) securing measured improvements in standards, or at least as compatible with such improvements. In this school the initiative was a recognised element of strategy following a disappointing inspection outcome, providing a means to build new strengths that both Ofsted and the local authority would recognise.
>
> (Ibid.)

We will return to this point in the conclusion of this chapter when we consider the key question of how we know whether a school is performing well in this area.

iii Ensure that the curriculum development is undertaken in a collaborative way

External partners will want to have a say in the development of the curriculum that you are putting together. The partnership will feel very one-sided if they are just presented with a finished curriculum document and there is little negotiation about its structure and content. But there is a balance here. External partners will have a broad range of other work that they will need to undertake; they will also normally look to you as the 'expert' in these matters and will expect you to take a lead.

However, remember that you are working collaboratively for a reason. All the potential benefits of partnership working within your locality need to be fostered. They will not just appear by accident! To take one example, let's imagine that you want to work collaboratively with a local employer. From your perspective, the perceived benefits might be that pupils will:

- Gain experience of a work environment;
- Understand more about the transition from school to adult life;

- Develop specific skills that will enrich their portfolio and help them construct a CV;
- Become more independent in their learning and take greater responsibility for it.

These benefits could form the basis of the conversation with the employer about the range and nature of the activities that could be offered to your pupils. Through conversation and discussion, they could eventually form the nucleus of some key learning objectives for the partnership and the accompanying curriculum (of which more below). Employers will know exactly how the work environment could help facilitate these skills in a general sense. However, in our experience, employers will often lack the skills and experience needed to plan for the development or sequential delivery of these skills through a structured piece of curriculum development. After all, this is not their day-to-day concern. But these are skills that you have and you will need to take a lead.

iv Ensure that parents are involved from start to finish

Partnership working is still quite new for many schools. Therefore, it is very important that parents are kept informed about new partnerships and how these are impacting on their child's education. As you will be aware, schools have standard procedures for liaising with parents. Make sure that new partnerships for learning are highlighted through regular communication via your school website, newsletter, emails or letters.

However, we would encourage you to think a bit further about involving and liaising with parents from the start to the finish of your project. From your perspective, the networks that your pupils' parents inhabit can be one of the most useful and productive source of potential new partnerships. Generally speaking, parents will naturally want to engage with you and ensure that their child is getting the best from their education. If they can be convinced about the benefits of partnership working then they will be much more likely to be receptive to approaches that the school might want to make to organisations and companies that they are working for or involved within.

The RSA project in Peterborough noted that this form of curriculum development can take time to set up and sustain, but that over time cultural change begins to take over and suddenly partnership working becomes a little more 'normal' within a local community. One teacher commented that:

> We've suddenly got to the place where if you mention partnership learning, there are quite a few people in Peterborough who now know what you mean. So if you ring up someone that you usually had a transaction with about a trip [she is] now aware that we want more than just a trip, and so can engage in that from her end as well. So I think that there's a bit of a culture shift.

This kind of self-perpetuating momentum will occur only if a school is committed to this way of working with a range of partners. It will not occur if the school is interested only in one-off projects. Parents remain an under-utilised resource in many schools. Building on their networks is a key to the creation of this kind of cultural change within a local community.

v Outside learning (or learning beyond the classroom)

There are strong arguments in favour of all pupils having a regular opportunity to learn outside the classroom as an integral part of their mainstream schooling. The Council for Learning Outside the Classroom believe that:

> Learning outside the classroom is about raising young people's achievement through an organised, powerful approach to learning in which direct experience is of prime importance. Meaningful learning occurs through acquiring skills through real life hands-on activities. This is not only about what we learn, but most importantly, how and where we learn.
>
> (LOTC 2012)

Many approaches to partnership working within an area-based curriculum development project will require you to take pupils out of their formal school environment and your classroom into the local area. This is not without its challenges! However, there has been a range of projects and initiatives in recent years that have provided schools with helpful support in this area. They tend to go under the banner of 'outside learning' or 'learning beyond the classroom'.

As a short aside, albeit one that is related to the main focus of this chapter, we will briefly consider some of the key issues involved in taking pupils outside of the school boundary.

First, be imaginative about your choices of outside learning opportunities. Organising a trip to an outside location can be very time-consuming and expensive. It is important to have a clear objective for the trip and to be able to justify this in terms of time and money.

Second, use the opportunity to engage in learning outside the normal classroom environment to help structure the teaching and learning opportunities prior to the trip and after it. Think about the various curriculum links and opportunities that such a trip will facilitate and integrate these in your broader unit of work.

Third, consider the various risks involved and seek the support of the member of staff at your school with a responsibility for health and safety issues when pupils are taking outside the normal school environment. There are also various legal responsibilities that you, and other teachers going on the trip, will need to ensure are met. This will include your having to prepare a full risk assessment.

Fourth, your school with have a 'charging policy' for school trips and you will need to find out what this is and how the trip can be financed properly to ensure all pupils can access it fairly.

Finally, you will need to communicate with your pupils' parents and carers well in advance of the trip itself. You will need their permission and you will want to ensure that they have a full understanding of the purposes for the trip in terms of the curriculum opportunities it offers their child.

2 Developing an area-based curriculum approach in your teaching: prioritising your pedagogy

Throughout the central part of this chapter we have discussed how important it is to work in partnership with your local community in the construction of an area-based curriculum model. We have stressed that this is best undertaken as part of a whole-school approach to curriculum development. However, we would now like to return to some of this chapter's opening themes about you and your work as an individual teacher. In particular, in the remainder of this chapter we will be focusing on things that are directly under your control and influence – principally your pedagogy.

At the opening of the chapter we introduced the work of Robin Alexander. We discussed his concept of pedagogy as discourse and pinpointed some of the key elements of this that related to this chapter's theme. Following on from this, Alexander introduces the notion of 'pedagogy as act':

> The core acts of teaching (task, activity, interaction and assessment) are framed by space, pupil organisation, time and curriculum, and by routines, rules and rituals. They are given form and are bounded temporally and conceptually by the lesson or teaching session.
>
> (Alexander 2004, p. 12)

This is where the pedagogical rubber hits the road. Decisions about issues such as how the space of classroom is organised, the timings of the lesson, the choice of activities or tasks, and the type and quality of interactions are all part of the 'pedagogy as act' concept. This is what the next part of this chapter will be exploring.

Practical task

Drawing on the Alexander's work on 'pedagogy as act', ask yourself questions about how these might influence your pedagogy in relation to a piece of area-based curriculum development. This is a significant task and we would not expect you to address all of these questions immediately. However, by taking a selection of these questions from the following examples you can begin to consider the consequences of adopting an area-based approach to curriculum development on your pedagogy. *Remember, there is no curriculum development without teacher development.*

SPACE

- How is my classroom *space* organised?
- How does this affect the quality of the *interactions* that occur between my pupils and I?
- How will my classroom space be extended (conceptually, virtually, geographically?) by adopting an area-based curriculum approach?

STUDENT ORGANISATION

- What are the common strategies I use to organise pupils?
- What would be the consequences of organising them in different ways (e.g. paired work instead of small group work)?
- How would these strategies need to be developed within an area-based approach to a unit of work?

TIME

- How do I organise the time within a typical lesson?
- How do I construct a balance between the common activities contained within a lesson?
- How will the adoption of an area-based approach to curriculum development result in any significant changes in how my lessons are structured and the time spent on various activities?

INTERACTION

- List the main types of interaction that occur within your lesson. These will not just be verbal.
- How do pupils interact with the tools you have chosen in the lesson (e.g. pieces of technology, textbooks, worksheets, etc.)?
- As I begin to work in partnership with others, how will these interactions being to develop?

RITUALS

- What are the *rituals* that are played out within my lesson?
- Where do these come from and are they productive?
- Is it within my power to change them?
- How will these change as I begin to implement an area-based curriculum approach?

An area-based curriculum has the potential to powerfully transform the pedagogy of the individual teacher. This can happen in numerous ways. Drawing on the framework provided by Robin Alexander, we will explore some of the key attributes of this below.

i Appreciating routines, rules and rituals

A new pedagogy for an area-based curriculum will build on the routines, rules and rituals of your classroom practice and wider school context. This 'building on' will take a number of forms. At its most extreme, it may see you replacing existing pedagogical elements within your teaching; less severely, you may be modifying your pedagogy by bringing in new features that will co-exist alongside existing elements of your practice; but, *and we think it is important to state this clearly*, there will be times in your teaching when the best way to teach will be through traditional subject-specific pedagogical approaches. Whatever you choose – replacement, modification, co-existence or no change – the point is that you are making a pedagogical choice. When thinking about a new area-based curriculum approach, the skillful element of the pedagogical choice relates to your perceptive analysis of the existing context (the routines, rules and rituals of your subject and school context).

ii Making coherent connections to the existing curriculum

As we explored in our consideration of the RSA's project in Peterborough, at each Key Stage within the primary and secondary curriculum there are frameworks within which teachers have to work. National Curriculum requirements, GCSE specifications or new diplomas all have key ingredients that impact on the way that you work. Within our consideration of the development of an area-based curriculum and pedagogy, there are some key principles worth considering.

First, an area-based curriculum approach should take a broader view of these frameworks, i.e. one that extends beyond the traditional subject boundary. This is quite a natural 'fit' given the key concepts that underpin this approach (i.e. a consideration of teaching and learning in a broader area or locality).

Springing from this wider viewpoint, the establishment of broader learning objectives within your teaching should be given freedom to develop. This is a good example of where 'co-existence' rather than 'replacement' is probably the best way forward. While you will have a responsibility to your own subject or phase, an area-based perspective will require you not just to be knowledgeable about what you are currently doing but also to plan for deliberate links between academic subjects and your local area in a constructive way. This will impact on your planning in various ways, notably on your setting of learning objectives.

It is worth reinstating some common advice about learning objectives here. One of the most frequent mistakes that young teachers make is that they write 'doing' objectives rather than 'learning' objectives. An example of a 'doing' objective is:

> Pupils will construct a three-dimensional representation of the house from the given two-dimensional drawings.

This describes the doing, the activity. It does not describe the learning that the pupils are engaging with while doing the activity. In this imaginary scenario, the learning might relate to developing a sense or appreciation of scale, representation or projection through the activity of constructing an accurate three-dimensional house from the two-dimensional drawings. The learning objective might read:

> Pupils will develop an understanding of scale and representation through considering the relationship between three-dimensional and two-dimensional images.

The linked learning outcomes may go into more detail about the activity, together with anticipated differentiated outcomes in terms of the learning that has or has not occurred.

Our argument here is that as long as these objectives are construed as doing objectives rather than learning objectives, the links to an area-based curriculum theme will remain difficult to establish. As a potential community partner not familiar with the Design and Technology curriculum, one might read the 'doing' objective in the above example and wonder what the purpose of the activity was. If I read the learning objective and saw the words 'scale', 'representation' and 'projection' then, perhaps, I could begin to make all kinds of imaginative links to my own context and work. The use of metaphorical connections such as this between subject knowledge and other settings is a powerful way of establishing links in a constructive way with others beyond your school community.

iii Utilising space constructively

For our discussion, space has two specific dimensions: curriculum space and physical space.

Curriculum space is allocated within timetables. The establishment of a timetable is a key informant and contributor to the notion of how schools operate, the subject boundaries that are established, and how specialism is valued. Within the majority of primary and secondary schools, teachers, pupils and parents expect subjects to be taught at a particular time and place. Subjects have become the organising component in most schools and the benefits of this approach are obvious. However, as we have seen already, the downside of this is that boundaries between subjects have been built up to such an extent that any alternative ways of working, of the type we are proposing here, are often difficult to facilitate without significant disruption. Larger-scale reconfigurations of the curriculum that avoid subjects being the sole organising principle of the school day have been experimented with by some schools (as an example, see the RSA's 'Manchester Curriculum Project', RSA 2009). However, this is far from normal in the majority of schools.

The creation of a new area-based unit of work, or even a full curriculum, will make significant demands on the curriculum planning within a school. While it might be slightly easier, logistically at least, to manage this within a primary school setting, the consequences of a major restructuring of the curriculum within a secondary school are significant and will need planning at least a year in advance.

But it is important to remember a key point here. An area-based curriculum approach of the type we have explored throughout our book will not always be something that requires such a significant reorganisation in terms of the curriculum itself. It can be conceived as a mindset, a way of thinking about your teaching, that can be implemented quite naturally within the day-to-day teaching that you are undertaking.

Physical space refers, obviously, to the classroom spaces within which you teach. There are many interesting stories of how new schools have been designed, together with innovative approaches to the design of individual learning spaces, from this project (Partnership for Schools 2010). But a quick survey of the types of learning spaces that a typical school contains makes the point that particular subjects have specific requirements in respect of physical spaces (e.g. science subjects are taught in laboratories; physical education requires the use of outdoor spaces, etc.).

So, for our discussion here, the argument moves from issues surrounding subject content to those surrounding subject pedagogy. To ask a science teacher to teach chemistry in a drama studio would challenge that teacher's way of thinking about their subject and how it is normally taught. Similarly, there is only so far that physical education can be taught in a traditional classroom setting. There are obvious and explicit requirements that both these subjects have (for laboratories and for the outdoors) that no one can, or should, deny.

The same is true when considering how to adopt an area-based approach to curriculum development and pedagogy. Extending or developing alternative spaces for learning, as well as bringing additional content to bear within the curriculum in existing spaces, will alternative the dynamics of teaching and learning in fundamental ways. There will be many positives here for your work and for your pupils. But you need to be aware of these differences so that you can build them into your curriculum design in an informed way.

iv The impact on short-, medium- and longer-term planning

In our opening chapter we made a general point that an area-based approach to curriculum development will impact on all three main areas of your planning as a teacher. This will include your lesson planning, your unit of work and longer-term planning. We have touched on elements of this throughout our book. The key point here is that you need to adopt an integrated approach to the specific themes of an area-based curriculum approach at each of the three levels. There needs to be an appropriate depth and breadth.

An important part of these considerations will be the opportunity to make links between teaching and learning that take place within and outside the classroom. As we considered above, the design of opportunities to relocate learning where possible and the creative use of homework activities could all become important parts of an enriched, area-based curriculum approach.

3 Developing an area-based curriculum approach in your teaching: planning a process of professional development

The third part of our discussion about developing an area-based curriculum approach in your teaching turns to the topic of professional development. Having considered the issues of partnerships and pedagogy, our discussion on professional development will present a simple model for moving your work forwards from this point.

There have been many studies of how teachers can improve their pedagogy (Altrichter *et al.* 1993; Edwards and Mercer 1987; Turner-Bisset 2001). For our purposes here, we will consider a model drawn from an interesting study of how a group of teachers' own professional development worked alongside a piece of collaborative curriculum development on which they were working. In this sense, the model serves to act as a bridge between this chapter's broader considerations about developing an area-based curriculum development model through partnerships and your own individual pedagogy.

Leat, Lofthouse and Taverner's study (2006) explored the patterns in teachers' thinking and conceptualised the conditions that supported the actions and interactions of a particular group of teachers who were seeking to implement what has recently become known as a 'thinking skills' curriculum. However, the focus of the study was not the piece of curriculum development itself, but rather the processes that the teachers went through as they developed their practice. From this analysis, the authors present a six-phased model.

Phase 1: Initiation

- Motivational aspects for proposed piece of curriculum development;
- Analysis of beliefs about teaching and learning;
- Identification of any external benefits for undertaking the development.

Phase 2: Novice

- Initial stage of teacher planning and classroom experimentation;
- Anxiety in planning lessons and preparing resources, but this can be overcome quickly.

Phase 3: Concerns

- Initial enthusiasm hits a buffer as the requirement for more detailed knowledge about pedagogical elements (e.g. an approach to questioning) become apparent;
- Self-doubts may emerge;
- Questioning the perceived benefits in relation to the amount of effort involved;
- Significant shifts in one's belief about teaching as the self-evaluation processes begin to challenge traditional thinking.

Phase 4: Consolidation

- Issues and concerns raised in the previous phase are resolved through collaboration and other external forms of support;
- Collaborative and comparative nature of the exercise helped staff maintain their energy and commitment;
- Sharing practice and related coaching was a significant benefit at this point;
- External benefits (e.g. studying for a higher degree) helped staff here.

Phase 5: Expansion

- Individual classroom practices began to make links across curricular subjects and with external themes;
- New practices gradually become embedded within routine practices;
- Further study aided this process.

Phase 6: Commitment

- Shift in teacher identity brought about by the opportunity to reflect on experiences and clarify beliefs;
- New practices embedded and no going back;
- Teachers become strong advocates of the innovation and sustain it in their own teaching.

When should a teacher be encouraged to adopt an area-based approach to curriculum development? We suggest that there are different answers that could be given to this question, depending on the teacher involved and the purposes behind the piece of curriculum development.

Teachers in the early stages of their career should be encouraged to adopt a broad perspective to their work as soon as possible. This should begin during their initial teacher education courses and carry across into their induction year. Although notions of subject knowledge and its application within pedagogy are contestable (Parker 2004; Parker and Heywood 2000), most young teachers will have degree-level knowledge in a subject area and will be keen to apply this in various different ways. The strategies for teaching in what might be called a centrifugal way, i.e. outward-looking in terms of their subject knowledge (Savage 2011), should be embedded strongly within the process of initial teacher education. This should include an area-based approach to curriculum development as part of a broader approach to cross-curricularity within their teaching.

Teachers who are further ahead in their careers have the benefit of experience and, providing that this has not resulted in complacency in terms of ongoing professional development, should allow them to enter the above model at a higher level. However, as with any change to one's pedagogy, it is likely that concerns will be felt when new approaches are implemented. Therefore, teachers within this category may feel significant challenges as subject-orientated approaches to teaching and learning begin to accommodate new area-based approaches to curriculum development.

In addition to the development of this approach within the work of an individual teacher, it is worth moving the focus away from them for a moment and to consider the wider, school-based systems that are needed in order to encourage and support this type of professional and curriculum development. We would agree with O'Brien and MacBeath (1999) that:

- Development will only be effective within a supportive, co-operative ethos at least at some level (school, department or classroom) but preferably at all levels;
- Those responsible for development must have a genuine understanding of the context in which teachers work – as teachers perceive it;
- Teachers need to be recognised as people at different stages in their personal and professional life cycle.

(O'Brien and MacBeath 1999, p. 70)

Working as a teacher can be a solitary experience at times. One of the benefits of this type of curriculum development is the opportunity to make productive links with other colleagues within the school and across a local community. This can be a powerful and motivating force and we would encourage you to explore these approaches further.

4 Developing an area-based curriculum approach in your teaching: practical steps to take your work forwards

Our fourth, and final, key point about developing an area-based curriculum approach for your teaching presents a range of practical steps that you can take to move your own work forwards in this exciting area of curriculum development. In doing so, we have borrowed explicitly from the excellent work done by the RSA in this area (which we have commented on throughout this chapter). This series of ideas is an elaboration on their framework as presented within their guide for practitioners (RSA 2012a, p. 21).

i Reflect

Ask yourself, or the school(s) with whom you are looking to work, the following three questions:

- Why is the local area important to the school curriculum?
- How open to change is the school curriculum?
- What, and who, 'counts' as local?

Put these questions to staff, partners, local employers, parents and anyone else involved.

Share the outcomes of the responses to these questions with all parties that you have canvassed opinions from. Use them to structure an ongoing debate with these partners as time allows.

ii Map

Take a serious look at what the area immediately around the school consists of, before looking further afield. What businesses, cultures, buildings, parks, streets, challenges and opportunities are there?

Map the school's existing connections to local business, people, parents and places to visit. How might these be used more fully? What kinds of relationships are they?

Ask pupils about their places of birth, family occupations and any international connections.

Ask pupils to place 'emoticons' on a physical map of the local area, indicating places about which they feel positively and negatively. This exercise can give you an excellent baseline in terms of how your pupils view their local area. It can help you evaluate the specific benefits of a particular project or intervention within your curriculum. We will consider this further in Chapter 9.

iii Engage

Engage early with partners, and begin a conversation about the purpose of education and the needs of the locality.

Be honest about the aims of everyone involved from the beginning, and address how those aims can be met.

Do not undervalue the skills and attributes that the school can bring to a partnership within an area-based curriculum project. Remember that the benefits of such a project flow both ways.

iv Scope

Have a wide-ranging scoping session that explores opportunities that are beyond the obvious. You can download a sample agenda for such a session here: www.thersa.org/action-research-centre/learning,-cognition-and-creativity/education/practical-projects/area-based-curriculum/reports-and-case-studies/project-tools.

In a wider school engagement, include as many staff as possible in this process. You could also engage selected partners from your community in this process.

v Plan

Make a concrete plan for a project together with a partner, including dates, learning objectives and key activities for your pupils. This should be similar to your standard medium-term, or unit of work, planning template.

Ensure that both parties are involved in the drafting of this plan and have a copy that they can refer to.

vi *Commit*

Draw up a partnership agreement which sets out the expectations on both parties. You can download a sample plan here: www.thersa.org/action-research-centre/ learning,-cognition-and-creativity/education/practical-projects/area-based-curriculum/ reports-and-case-studies/project-tools.

Conclusion: how does a school know if it is doing well?

This chapter has explored a range of issues associated with the development of an area-based curriculum and pedagogy. It has focused primarily on your work as an individual teacher and considered how you can develop and adapt your pedagogy to facilitate this approach. We have also looked in some detail at the nature of partnerships that could characterise an extended, perhaps whole-school, way of working in this area.

We would encourage you to share and discuss ideas regarding the development of an area-based curriculum with your senior managers. One of the roles of senior managers in schools should be to support and develop platforms for these types of discussion between colleagues. More widely, they (and you) should be encouraged to tell your stories of curriculum developments to wider audiences, including Ofsted, and it is the role of policy-makers to value, promote and find ways to facilitate this kind of curriculum development.

This begs an important question: what do we mean when we say that a school is doing well? For some, the results of publicly tested examinations are one of the key measurements of a school's success. Eisner, reporting on the situation in the United States of America, writes that:

> Tests [have] come to define our priorities. And now we have legitimated those priorities by talking about 'core subjects'. The introduction of the concept of core subjects explicitly marginalizes subjects that are not part of the core.... Our idea of core subjects is related to our assessment practices and the tests we use to determine whether or not schools are doing well.
>
> (Eisner 2009, p. 329)

The consequences of such a positioning are well known to us in the United Kingdom:

> The message that we send to pupils is that what really matters in their education are their test scores. As a result, pupils in high-stakes testing programs find ways to cut corners – and so do some teachers. We read increasingly often not only about pupils who are cheating but also about teachers who are unfairly helping pupils get higher scores on the tests. It's a pressure that undermines the kind of experience that pupils ought to have in schools.
>
> (Ibid., pp. 329–330)

Is this a little strong? Sadly, these pressures are only too well understood by teachers. In 2012, a poll by the Association of Teachers and Lecturers found that 35 per cent of teachers said that they could be persuaded to cheat in this way (Shepherd 2012). More recently, Fiona Miller has reported that it is time to accept that some schools are routinely cheating and that action needs to be taken to preserve the integrity of the education system for the majority of schools that play by the rules (Miller 2013).

Eisner's answer to the question 'what do we mean when we say that a school is doing well?' is multi-faceted but is built around the importance of us, as a society, developing a wider appreciation for the work of schools beyond the scores that pupils obtain through standardised testing mechanisms such as SATS or the GCSE examination. One of the key elements of this concerns the main theme of our chapter – the establishment of broader approaches to an area-based curriculum and pedagogy.

Eisner writes:

> What connections are pupils helped to make between what they study in class and world outside of school? A major aim of education has to do with what psychologists refer to as 'transfer of learning'. Can pupils apply what they have learned or what they have learned how to learn? Can they engage in the kind of learning they will need in order to deal with problems and issues outside of the classroom? If what pupils are learning is simply used as a means to increase their scores on the next test, we may win the battle and lose the war. In such a context, school learning becomes a hurdle to jump over.... The really important dependent variables in education are not located in classrooms. Nor are they located in schools. The really important dependent variables are located outside schools. Our assessment practices haven't even begun to scratch that surface. It's what pupils do with what they learn when they can do what they want to do that is the real measure of educational achievement.
>
> (Eisner 2009, p. 331)

As with so much of Eisner's writing, he puts his finger right on the key point in a direct way. Has your school reduced knowledge to 'subjects', and teaching to 'mere telling' (Alexander 2008, p. 141)? Educating our children is too important to be left to schools alone. It is for this reason that an area-based approach to curriculum development and pedagogy is so important. It challenges us as teachers to raise our vision beyond our immediate classroom and to focus on the broader context within which our pupils' lives are located. It forces us to rethink our pedagogy at a fundamental level and it invites us to relocate our curriculum within a collaboration or partnership with significant others in our community. Eisner's chapter closes with some important questions that we will raise here as our chapter reaches its end. Please consider these very seriously:

- Can we widen what parents and others believe to be important in judging the quality of our schools?
- Can we widen and diversify what they think matters?
- Can those of us who teach think about education not only as the education of the public in the schools (i.e. our pupils) but also as the education of the public outside of our schools (i.e. parents and community members)?

- Can a more substantial and complex understanding of what constitutes good schooling contribute to better, more enlightened support for our schools?

(Ibid.)

References

Alexander, R. J. (2004) 'Still No Pedagogy? Principle, pragmatism and compliance in primary education'. *Cambridge Journal of Education* 34:1, pp. 7–34.
Alexander, R. J. (2008) *Essays on Pedagogy*. London, Routledge.
Altrichter, H., Posch, P. and Somekh, B. (1993) *Teachers Investigate Their Work*. London, Routledge.
Edwards, D. and Mercer, N. (1987) *Common Knowledge: The development of understanding in the classroom*. London, Methuen.
Eisner, E. (2009) 'What Does it Mean to Say a School is Doing Well?' In Flinders, D. and Thornton, S. (eds) (2009) *The Curriculum Studies Reader*. London, Routledge, pp. 327–335.
Goodson, I. F. and Mangen, J. M. (1998). 'Subject Cultures and the Introduction of Classroom Computers'. In Goodson, I. F. (ed.) *Subject Knowledge: Readings for the study of school subjects*. London, Falmer Press.
Jephcote, M. and Davies, B. (2007) 'School Subjects, Subject Communities and Curriculum Change: The social construction of economics in the school curriculum'. *Cambridge Journal of Education* 37:2, pp. 207–227.
Kushner, S. (1993) 'One in a Million? The individual at the centre of quality control'. In Elliott, J. (ed.) *Reconstructing Teacher Education: Teacher development*. London, Falmer Press, pp. 39–50.
Leat, D., Lofthouse, R. and Taverner, S. (2006) 'The Road Taken: Professional pathways in innovative curriculum development'. *Teachers and Teaching: Theory and practice* 12:6, pp. 657–674.
LOTC (Council for Learning Outside the Classroom) (2012) www.lotc.org.uk [last accessed 18 February 2014].
Miller, F. (2013) 'Radical Action is Needed Now to Stop Schools Cheating at GCSEs'. www.the-guardian.com/education/2013/sep/09/schools-gcse-exam-cheats [last accessed 24 March 2014].
O'Brien, J. and MacBeath, J. (1999) 'Co-ordinating Staff Development: The training and development of staff development co-ordinators'. *Journal of In-service Education* 25, pp. 69–83.
Parker, J. (2004) 'The Synthesis of Subject and Pedagogy for Effective Learning and Teaching in Primary Science Education'. *British Educational Research Journal* 30:6, pp. 819–839.
Parker, J. and Heywood, D. (2000) 'Exploring the Relationship between Subject Knowledge and Pedagogic Content Knowledge in Primary Teachers' Learning about Forces'. *International Journal of Science Education* 22:1, pp. 89–111.
Partnership for Schools (2010) 'Library'. www.partnershipsforschools.org.uk/library/library.jsp [last accessed 5 January 2010].
Peshkin, A. (1988) 'In Search of Subjectivity – One's Own'. *Educational Researcher* 17:7, pp. 17–22.
Peshkin, A. (1991) *The Color of Strangers, the Color of Friends: The play of ethnicity in school and community*. Chicago, University of Chicago Press.
RSA (Royal Society for the encouragement of Arts, Manufactures and Commerce) (2009) *Manchester Curriculum: A report and reflections for further development*. London, RSA.
RSA (2012a) *Thinking About an Area-based Curriculum: A guide for practitioners*. London, RSA. Also available from www.thersa.org/action-research-centre/learning,-cognition-and-creativity/education/practical-projects/area-based-curriculum/reports-and-case-studies/thinking-about-an-area-based-curriculum-a-guide-for-practitioners [last accessed 24 March 2014].

RSA (2012b) *Learning About, By and For Peterborough: The RSA area-based curriculum in Peterborough*. London, RSA.

Savage, J. (2011) *Cross-curricular Teaching and Learning in the Secondary School*. London, Routledge.

Shepherd, J. (2012) 'Teachers tempted to rewrite pupils' exam answers'. www.theguardian.com/education/2012/apr/02/teachers-under-pressure-to-cheat [last accessed 24 March 2014].

Stenhouse, L. (1975) *An Introduction to Curriculum Research and Development*. London, Heinemann Educational.

Turner-Bisset, R. (2001) *Expert Teaching*. London, David Fulton.

Chapter 7

Local and personal learning networks

Throughout this book we have argued that teachers are central to the development of the curriculum; they are the curriculum makers. Curriculum development is inextricably linked to teacher development. Sharing is integral to effective teaching. As teachers we share many things. But how is sharing linked to the development of a community such as that found within your classroom or school and how does this relate to your local area? How can you develop a personal and professional network that allows you to engage with others and share productively?

This chapter will explore these and other related issues. Within it, we will argue that the construction of a personal learning network is central to your work as a teacher. By doing so, you will be able to reach out into your local area and form productive relationships that will inform your own curriculum planning and the development of area-based curricula. This chapter focuses on you and your individual work; the next chapter will explore how these can develop further through explicit partnership approaches to educational provision.

Reflective task

What does sharing mean to you as a teacher? Again, make a list but then try to place your ideas into groups. What sharing is about knowledge? What is about skills? What is related to attitudes or personality? What else comes under the umbrella of 'sharing'?

The mill and the market

Will lives in a small town outside of Wigan. In the early 1900s this was a mill town. The major cotton mills of the area not only dominated the landscape and silhouetted the evening skyline, but were also the principal context within which people shared their lives. The mill buildings, chimneys and associated facilities that physically connected all this must have made quite an impression at this time. They rose high into the air, dominating the sky with an eerie presence.

The mill employed most of the habitants of the local area. People shared knowledge, skills and experiences; they brought what knowledge they had to the area, to their work and homes, and shared this in a reciprocal manner. The process of learning at the mill was a process of sharing skills. Then, after the hours of work, people shared, helped, provided each other with skills, learnt from each other. Skills such as dressmaking, baking, working with metal or wood were commodities; something that could be 'traded'. People who lived and worked in this manner thrived; others who brought less to the 'skills table' found it more difficult to get on. They often moved on to other areas or to other types of work.

These communities were close-knit. People knew each other, the mills looked more like large villages, and within this village was all you needed for life. The housing was built for the workers; they had shared walls, gardens and windows that faced each other. Community was at the heart of this life. That is not to say that times were not hard, but people were known to each other, they supported each other, they found a sense of identity in the jobs that they did and the skills that they provided to the wider community.

Over the last 100 years things have changed significantly. Perhaps the picture painted above is a little idyllic. But, despite these changes, there are many elements of our lives together that resonate with the community that lived and worked together within a mill town. There are numerous examples. Jonathan lives in Sandbach, a medium-sized market town in south Cheshire. Within the town there is a successful amateur rugby club. One of Jonathan's sons is a member of one of the youth teams. The rugby club is a community within itself. It comprises a couple of hundred children and young people, and their associated immediate and extended families. Rugby as a sport crosses many social barriers. Spending time within the rugby club connects people together. You will find roofers, builders, writers, journalists, health professionals, educators and many other rubbing shoulders on the touch line (and the bar afterwards). A common passion for a sport becomes a starting point for trade, services and skills shared within the local community of Sandbach.

Both the examples of the mill and the market town, despite being separated by over 100 years, demonstrate the centrality of networks to our lives. We are social beings and the ways in which we are connected to our local area are a central part of our psychology and well-being. Throughout this book, we have argued, because of this imperative, that it is vitally important to make connections between the formal process of schooling and education and the locality within which one's school is located and where its pupils live. Defining one's personal and professional learning network is an important practical step that you can take to ensure that your work as a teacher is contextualised appropriately within your locality.

At a simple level, a network is a series of connections through which things are shared. From roads, which join towns together, to virtual networks, which join us in our online communities, networks are connectives that join us together as people and as a society. From families to friends to colleagues to neighbours, we are all connected in a series of networks. These networks connect where we live to whom we live near and then more widely across our region, country and world.

One of the most famous networks is the London Underground system. The diagrammatic representation of the various tube lines has an interesting history.

Harry Beck was a technical draughtsman who worked in the London Underground in the signalling office. In his spare time during the early 1930s he began to draw maps of the underground. As part of his work maintaining the signals, he often had to deal with the very complex maps that there were of this subterranean travel system. These maps, with their curved lines, precise geographical representation and accurate distances, were extremely complicated. What Beck realised was that the accuracy of the map in relation to the actual distances between stations, the exact shape of the connections and their relationship to overground features was not important. What people needed was just the order of the stations and where connections to other lines could be made. This enabled them to understand the system. It enabled them to navigate the complex network.

Beck's map, finally published in 1933, was not initially well received but, as anyone knows who has travelled on the London Underground since, has become an iconic symbol for London in modern times. What was so brilliant about Beck's idea was that he realised that underground, only the sequence of stations and where they joined each other was important. He had simplified the network into its essential items. This is vital in the understanding the use of networks. In the language of network science, topology is more important than metrics. Not only was the new map much easier to use, it changed the way people moved in and around London and even, it can be argued, helped create the suburbs of the capital by making them look closer to the centre, thereby encouraging people to move there.

Reflective task

Take some time to write down the networks that inform your teaching. Who do you work with? What networks are you involved in? What networks are your school involved in? How is your curriculum a network? Where does it connect?

Then try to sketch this out. Try to simplify the 'map' as Beck did. Try to consider:

*   Your school curriculum: how is it formed, by whom, driven by what?
*   Your subject and how it is taught;
*   Your pupils and their lives both within and beyond the school boundary;
*   People who have been, or are, influential to your thinking about education;
*   Key organisations you engage with regularly;
*   Processes of professional development or performance management;
*   Your local area and how it implicates and informs your work.

Developing your own personal learning network

The construction of a personal learning network is key to your development of an approach to teaching and learning that begins in your classroom and spans outwards into your local community and beyond. As with any element of the subject or subjects that you teach, or the pedagogical knowledge that you utilise to do this well, knowing about the tools, techniques and technologies that professionals employ in various spheres to construct, use and evaluate their personal learning networks are vital. But, before we turn our attention to those, what is a personal learning network?

1 Defining a personal learning network

A personal learning network is the way that you organise your learning through connections with social and information networks. It will contain a number of different things, including tools that help you organise your work, e.g. using Evernote to store ideas, Scrivener to write lesson materials, or Moodle to host educational materials. However, these tools in and of themselves are not a personal learning network. Personal learning networks go beyond the organisational and help you develop new knowledge, information and skills through engagement with others and their ideas. In other words, a personal learning network is a social network as well as a purely informational or organisational network. It will involve you making connections within your own personal circle of friends, your colleagues, school, local community and far beyond that too!

Practical task

Have a look at diagrammatic representations of personal learning networks that some teachers have published online, for example the following (all last accessed 25 November 2014):

- www.cats-pyjamas.net/2012/04/one-way-to-grow-a-networked-teacher-is-to-grow-a-networked-learner-pln/
- www.teachersusingtech.weebly.com/personal-learning-networks.html
- www.slideshare.net/caspamajola/my-personal-learning-network-diagram

For each one, try and identify the key elements in terms of people, tools, information or other key sources.

As the examples in the above practical task clearly show, there is an emphasis on the word 'personal' in the phrase 'personal learning networks'! This comes across in the ways in which people have chosen to represent their networks in graphic form as well as the actual content within each one. Your own personal learning network is going to look slightly different from anyone else's network. What key elements did you notice? We found the following key ingredients:

- People, including your colleagues at school, your family and other members of your community: all of these folk will have an input into your network and will be a support for your teaching;
- Print resources, including books, articles, journals and other writing;
- Curriculum documents, including examination specifications, handbooks, course materials and the like: all of these will contain useful prompts, hints and tips for your teaching;
- Broader communication tools such as email, direct messaging and video conferencing, all of which can help you stay connected to others within your network;
- Key archives of information such as Wikipedia, other wikis, YouTube and photo-sharing sites;
- Curated collections of teaching resources within spaces such as slide-sharing sites, Google docs or similar hosted environments;
- Online networked communities such as Facebook, LinkedIn and Plurk, which help you find and connect with new people according to shared professional interests or shared materials.

2 Competences and personal learning networks

A personal learning network is more than a collection of tools. However, in contrast to the communities built around the old mill towns, or even the physical networks built around local clubs or societies today such as Sandbach Rugby Club, there is one massive network that the vast majority of us use every day to engage with others: the web! Understanding how the web works and developing our competence with digital tools to use it constructively will help you develop a personal learning network that you can use to inform and develop your teaching.

Auditing your competence in this area is an important first step towards developing new skills. After all, if you do not know where your strengths and weaknesses are, how can you constructively seek to improve yourself? Fortunately, many large companies such as Microsoft, Mozilla and Google provide frameworks to help you explore your own web competencies in various ways. One of the most helpful, in our experience, is provided by Mozilla, the creators of the Firefox web browser.

Practical task

As part of their work to support education, Mozilla have produced a set of competencies and skills that they (and their stakeholders) believe are important to pay attention to and get better at as you read, write and participate on the web (Mozilla 2014). These competences and skills are listed under three main headings: exploring, building and connecting. We have copied the full list of competencies and skills below. Why not use them as an audit of your own skills and competence in these areas. Which areas are you strong in? Which areas do you need to broaden your skills or competence within? Which are most important for teaching in your opinion?

EXPLORING

Navigation: *Using software tools to browse the web.*

- Accessing the web using the common features of web browsers;
- Using hyperlinks to access a range of resources on the web;
- Reading, evaluating, and manipulating URLs;
- Recognising the visual cues in everyday web services;
- Using browser add-ons and extensions to provide additional functionality.

Web mechanics: *Understanding the web ecosystem.*

- Using and understanding the differences between URLs, IP addresses and search terms;
- Managing information from various sources on the web;
- Demonstrating the difference between the results of varying search strategies.

Search: *Locating information, people and resources via the web.*

- Using keywords, search operators, and keyboard shortcuts to make web searches more efficient;
- Finding real-time or time-sensitive information using a range of search techniques;
- Locating or finding desired information within search results;
- Synthesising information found from online resources through multiple searches.

Credibility: *Critically evaluating information found on the web.*

- Making judgements based on technical and design characteristics to assess the credibility of information;
- Researching authorship and ownership of websites and their content;
- Comparing information from a number of sources to judge the trustworthiness of content;
- Discriminating between 'original' and derivative web content.

Security: *Keeping systems, identities, and content safe.*

- Detecting online scams and 'phishing' by employing recognised tools and techniques;
- Encrypting data and communications using software and add-ons;
- Changing the default behavior of websites, add-ons and extensions to make web browsing more secure.

BUILDING

Composing for the web: *Creating and curating content for the web.*

- Inserting hyperlinks into a web page;
- Embedding multimedia content into a web page;
- Creating web resources in ways appropriate to the medium/genre;
- Identifying and using HTML tags;
- Structuring a web page.

Remixing: *Modifying existing web resources to create something new.*

- Identifying and using openly-licensed work;
- Combining multimedia resources;
- Creating something new on the web using existing resources.

Design and accessibility: *Creating universally effective communications through web resources.*

- Identifying the different parts of a web page using industry-recognised terms;
- Improving the accessibility of a web page by modifying its colour scheme and markup;
- Iterating on a design after feedback from a target audience;
- Reorganising the structure of a web page to improve its hierarchy/conceptual flow;
- Demonstrating the difference between inline, embedded and external CSS;
- Using CSS tags to change the style and layout of a web page.

Coding/scripting: *Creating interactive experiences on the web.*

- Explaining the differences between client-side and server-side scripting;
- Composing working loops and arrays;

- Reading and explaining the structure of code;
- Using a script framework;
- Adding code comments for clarification and attribution.

Infrastructure: *Understanding the Internet stack.*

- Understanding and labelling the web stack;
- Explaining the differences between the web and the Internet;
- Exporting and backing up your data from web services;
- Moving the place(s) where your data is hosted on the web;
- Securing your data against malware and computer criminals.

CONNECTING

Sharing: *Creating web resources with others.*

- Sharing a resource using an appropriate tool and format for the audience;
- Tracking changes made to co-created web resources;
- Using synchronous and asynchronous tools to communicate with web communities, networks and groups.

Collaborating: *Providing access to web resources.*

- Choosing a web tool to use for a particular contribution/collaboration;
- Co-creating web resources;
- Configuring notifications to keep up-to-date with community spaces and interactions.

Community participation: *Getting involved in web communities and understanding their practices.*

- Encouraging participation in web communities;
- Using constructive criticism in a group or community setting;
- Configuring settings within tools used by online communities;
- Participating in both synchronous and asynchronous discussions;
- Expressing opinions appropriately in web discussions;
- Defining different terminology used within online communities.

Privacy: *Examining the consequences of sharing data online.*

- Identifying rights retained and removed through user agreements;
- Taking steps to secure non-encrypted connections;
- Explaining ways in which computer criminals are able to gain access to user information;
- Managing the digital footprint of an online persona;
- Identifying and taking steps to keep important elements of identity private.

Open practices: *Helping to keep the web democratic and universally accessible.*

- Distinguishing between open and closed licensing;
- Making web resources available under an open licence;
- Using and sharing files in open, web-friendly formats when appropriate;
- Contributing to an Open Source project.

(Mozilla 2014)

As we read through these points we had our own views about which related best to our teaching. Clearly, some of the competencies have specific applications within technical contexts that might not be relevant to your work. But the vast majority of these skills will touch on your work as a teacher in some way.

When you have completed the audit of your skills, you should be able to identify those areas that need strengthening or developing. This is where the resource is most powerful. For each of the key competence areas Mozilla have produced a set of training materials to help you develop that skill further. Here, we will briefly consider 'Navigation' as one of the simpler competences; after all, we can all use a web browser – right?

As with our competence with any tool, we can all learn to use a web browser more skilfully. For most of us, a web browser is the software that we use to interface with and explore the web. Given that we are all busy people with loads to do every day, sharpening and developing our skills of navigation with a web browser will make us, and our teaching, more productive. Within the help section devoted to 'Navigation' (https://webmaker.org/en-US/resources/literacy/weblit-Navigation), we are given an overview of what a web browser can help us do (under the heading of 'Discover'), a summary of the key skills that we will develop in order to use it better, and, most importantly, tips about how to shape and mould the tool (in this case, the web browser) to our specific requirements as a teacher (under the heading of 'Make'). The final section of the help resource is 'Teach'. Here, you, and other teachers, can access and submit helpful materials to help contextualise the knowledge, skills and understanding of this particular web competence for yourself and others.

While Mozilla are not the only company that are producing this kind of educational guide to web competencies, we have found this set of resources to be particularly helpful and would highly recommend them to you as you begin to build your own skills and create your own personal learning network.

Auditing your web competencies, using a framework of ideas and support materials such as those provided within resources put together by Mozilla, is an important first step in building a personal learning network. When people think about building a personal learning network online they tend immediately to think of tools. The problem is the plethora of desktop-based, portable, mobile and web-based tools that already exists and the number of tools that are being introduced to that list on a weekly basis. It is very easy to drown in tool overload! Resources such as Mozilla's toolkit emphasise the importance of developing skills and appropriate understanding around key competencies rather than focusing primarily on the tools themselves.

3 Behaviour within a personal learning network

To put it another way, building a personal learning network to help underpin and inform your teaching is not about adopting specific tools (although specific tools of the type we will explore later in this chapter will be important). It is more about a mind-set or set of behaviours that you need to identify, adopt and apply to your work as a teacher.

Howard Rhinegold is a leading critic, writer and teacher who has thought hard about social and pedagogical implications of using social media in this way. In his eight tweets written in 2011, Rhinegold identified a set of key behaviours that we can adopt and expand on here to help you begin the construction of your own approach to a personal learning network. The eight 'behaviours' that Rhinegold identified in his tweets were:

- *Explore*: it is not just about knowing how to find experts, co-learners, but about exploration to serendipitous encounter;
- *Search*: use Diigo, Delicious, Listorius to find pools of expertise in the fields that interest you;
- *Follow* candidates through RSS, Twitter. Ask yourselves over days, weeks whether each candidate merits continued attention;
- Always keep *tuning* your network, dropping people who don't gain sufficiently high interest; adding new candidates;
- *Feed* the people who follow you if you come across information that you suspect would interest them;
- *Engage* the people you follow. Be mindful of making demands on their attention;
- *Enquire* of the people you follow, of the people who follow you;
- *Respond* to enquiries made to you. Contribute to both diffuse reciprocity and quid pro quo. (These tweets were curated by Alex Howard into Storify at: https://storify.com/digiphile/how-to-build-a-personal-learning-network-on-twitter.)

Whatever tools you decide to utilise within your personal learning network, these behaviours are vital ones to cultivate as you begin to expand your teaching in a local context. How will they apply to your work as a teacher? We will briefly explore each one below in a reflective task together with some questions to prompt your own thinking.

Reflective task

A EXPLORING

According to Rhinegold, exploration is an invitation to serendipitous encounter. It is important to be open to new ideas about your teaching and to give yourself the best opportunity to encounter new ideas and knowledge about how you can teach better. These ideas can come from various sources including, as we will consider in our next chapter, through working in partnership with others. But one of the key skills in terms of the digital dimension of your teaching and learning network is being able to recognise the opportunities inherent within your exploration online. Developing that ability to recognise potential and apply it to your own work takes time but is worth cultivating. Being 'explorative' is one of the key skills of being an effective teacher.

Key questions:

- How can I be more receptive and open to new ideas about teaching?
- How can my personal learning network help me explore the opportunities inherent within my contact with new teachers, their ideas about teaching and how it can be done differently?

B SEARCHING

Searching productively is linked to exploring. As we will discuss below, there are a large range of tools available for you to use here. Searching involves finding interesting stuff but also capturing and curating it sensibly so you can access it when needed. It is easy to get swamped with too many digital, as well as physical, resources. In terms of building a personal learning network, one of your principal aims here is to identify key people and sources of informative, engaging and provocative thinking about teaching that will help you develop your own thinking and pedagogy further.

Key questions:

- What tools do I use already to help me search for new information or people?
- What do I do with the interesting information that I find?
- How do I use the things I find to help develop my own pedagogy?

C FOLLOWING

If you have been able to explore and search productively, you will have found key people and key sources of ideas that you will need to follow. Your personal learning network is beginning to grow! At this point you will need to be quite critical. It is easy for your network to grow too quickly and become too noisy (i.e. there is too much 'stuff' there and it becomes difficult for you to see the wood for the trees). This is particularly true for you as a teacher. You do not have the luxury of time on your hands. Presumably there are other things that you'd like to do as well as teach!

It is also too easy to surround your network with comforting voices that underpin your own viewpoint. Although there is nothing intrinsically wrong with this, it will be important for you to follow people or sources of information that provide challenge to your own thinking (think 'grit' within an oyster that produces a pearl!). Therefore, you will regularly need to ask some hard questions about the people and sources within your personal learning network.

Key questions:

- Is this person or source providing high-quality information that I am finding useful within my personal learning network?
- Are the key messages from any one person or source targeted specifically? Or is there too much 'noise' around their feed of information that makes it difficult for me to ascertain what is valuable?

- Is there an appropriate degree of challenge to my own way of thinking from my sources?

D TUNING

Tuning your personal learning network is a vital behaviour and needs to be done regularly. Think about this in relationship to an old analogue radio signal within a car radio. While it might work perfectly in one area, as you travel across the country it gradually weakens and gets noisier until it is lost completely. It will need retuning, manually or automatically, to maintain its signal quality. The same is true within a personal learning network. You will need to evaluate your key sources over time. As the power of any one specific source fades you will need to either retune or delete that signal in favour of another. Having too many tired or weak signals will just weigh down your network and mean that key messages are hidden within too much background noise.

Key questions:

- Is the quality of input from my key people or sources being maintained over time?
- What adjustments do I need to make to my personal learning network in order to maintain its clarity and usefulness?

E FEEDING

Feeding is about building relationships with others within your personal learning network. Up to this point, we have put you at the centre of the network. Through the key behaviours of exploring, searching, following and tuning, we have argued that you can build a personal learning network that benefits you and your teaching. Feeding is about giving stuff out to your network rather than just receiving stuff in. Here, basic aspects of human communication apply. As you make contact and share interesting stuff, people will respond and share good stuff with you! As you are open and generous with your time and resources, so you will find that others will be towards you too. This is true in our day-to-day relationships with fellow teachers and our students too.

The key point here that Rhinegold is at pains to emphasise is that you need to be proactive within your personal learning network. Share first. Do not wait for someone you are connected with to share something with you. Take the initiative. Give and things will be given to you. Become known as someone who gives more than they receive within your network. This is the key to creating a rich personal learning network of your own.

Key questions:

- What can I share within my personal learning network?
- How can I be more generous with my own ideas and resources about teaching within my network?

F ENGAGING

Engaging goes beyond feeding and giving. It is about using your personal learning network to go beyond basic sharing of ideas and information to share insights and experiences at a deeper level with those that you trust. Rhinegold's work here reminds us of the importance of being kind and courteous in our engagement with others. Many of our interactions online are done through words (although increasingly image and video are coming into play). When we cannot see someone in cyberspace, words like 'please' and 'thank you' are vitally important in our communication and will really mark you out as a teacher who is wanting to engage seriously with others. As importantly, they will help create a learning network that it is enjoyable to spend time within.

Key questions:

- What are the hallmarks of a quality communication and engagement with someone online?
- How can I build on the strengths of my own communication with others in the 'real' world and ensure that high standards are maintained within my engagement with others online?

G ENQUIRING

Feeding and engaging with the ideas of other teachers within your personal learning network are the first level of interaction. Enquiring and responding (see below) can be conceptualised as a second level of communication or interaction. Enquiring about others and their well-being builds value in our online relationships. Clearly this is as true in our face-to-face relationships. Being mindful about others and their work will enrich your personal learning network and, as we saw in our discussion around feeding your network, will result in a richer form of communication and support for yourself as a result.

Key questions:

- How can I build time into my working life to enquire about others and their work within my own personal learning network?
- How do the basic human interactions that I have developed over time in my face-to-face relationships translate into a personal learning network where others are, in one sense, more remote and the standard forms of expression do not apply so easily?

H RESPONDING

Responding appropriately to others within your personal learning network is Rhinegold's final suggestion for us to consider. As people engage with you and enquire about your work, be responsive and take the opportunity to build strong and meaningful connections with others. If someone takes the time to write a comment on your blog, acknowledge it and thank them and, more than that, engage with their points in a constructive way. Build capacity and strength in that particular node of your personal learning network. It will never be time wasted. But as important as the content of the message is the way that it is transmitted. Ensure that you set a good example and influence your network with a positive tone at all times.

Key questions:

- What kind of responses would I like to receive from the enquiries that I make within my personal learning network? How can I model these in my own responses to others who contact me?

- More broadly, how can I set a good example for others within my personal learning network?

4 Tools to help develop your personal learning network

In the previous section we used eight key words drawn from the work of Howard Rhinegold to discuss the broad range of behaviours that we will need to adopt to build a positive and productive personal learning network. At this point, it is probably a good idea to remember that the best personal learning networks are blends of the online and offline. Many of the eight behaviours described above are just as applicable to physical networks and partnerships that underpin your teaching. We will be exploring this further in the next chapter.

In this section we are going to consider some of the most common tools that you could use to help build a personal learning network of your own. Rhinegold's own thinking in this area has informed the development of a 'social media classroom and collaboratory' that includes various tools such as forums, blogs, wikis, chat rooms, social bookmarking tools and loads of other stuff alongside standard curriculum materials and resources (http://socialmediaclassroom.com/index.php/). It is an interesting example of how one leading educator has built and curated a personal learning network from a set of standard tools.

While such a curated set of tools might be a good starting point for your work, we are going to suggest that you go back to some basics as you begin your personal learning network. We have tried and tested all of the following tools and found them to be useful core components to our work as educators. Clearly, you will to make your own choices but we would highly recommend the following tools, which are all accessible and usable from desktop and mobile technologies.

i Your web browser: the most important choice for exploring, searching and connecting

Your web browser is probably your most important tool in your personal learning network. It is your interface with the web and probably the one piece of software that you will spend more time looking at than anything else! Every web browser has its own set of strengths and weaknesses. When choosing a browser, there are a number of key questions and options that you will want to consider:

- What is the best browser for speed?
- What is the best browser for add-ons and functionality?
- What is the best browser in terms of the other software that I have on my computer or mobile device (e.g. Windows, Mac OS, etc.)?
- What is the best browser in terms of the hardware that I am using?
- What is the best browser in terms of the privacy that it affords?
- Increasingly, for the immediate future, what is the best browser in terms of its compliance with HTML5 and the affordances that this will offer for future online applications?

Whatever browser you do choose, there will be opportunities for you to personalise it to your own specific requirements. You can do this through the incorporation of add-ons and bookmarks. These might include applications from other tools within the personal learning network (e.g. an Evernote web clipper) or bespoke applications in their own right (e.g. Zotero, a research tool that allows you to collect, organise and share online content simply).

ii Twitter (www.twitter.com): exploring, following and engaging

Twitter has become one of the most powerful online tools. Its applications are far too numerous for us to explore here and but perhaps its core strength is in its ability to easily connect people and their ideas together in short fragments of text, image or video. Twitter is, perhaps, a personal learning network all on its own and all of the behaviour traits that we have explored above are relevant to its use. However, for us it is just one part of a wider selection of tools that you will need to adopt.

iii WordPress (www.wordpress.com): feeding, sharing and responding

WordPress is a content management system that has, in recent years, become a world-leading platform for bloggers. There are managed WordPress installations at sites such as www.wordpress.com or you can host your own domain on your own server. Blogging provides you with that time and space to explore ideas and share resources without the 140-word limit imposed by Twitter. Whether through a self-hosted or managed account, the functionality offered by WordPress (and the various ways in which you can extend this through plugins) make it an essential and core part of a personal learning network.

iv Evernote (www.evernote.com): collecting, curating and sharing

Evernote is the ultimate digital scrapbook. It allows you to write notes, collect things like clippings from web pages, images or video, tag everything and then share it with others. It is a brilliant way to keep track of everything that you need in terms of teaching resources, new ideas for curriculum development, pieces of classroom research or evaluation that you are undertaking, or materials for students to access outside of your formal lessons. Evernote produce another tool called Skitch (www.evernote.com/skitch) that allows you to annotate anything that you have collected simply and easily. It has wonderful applications as a teaching tool.

v Scrivener (www.literatureandlatte.com/scrivener.php): writing, curating and preparing

This book has been written with Scrivener. Many of the world's leading novelists and playwrights, journalists, lawyers and academics use Scrivener. But why is it included here as core tool for a personal learning network?

Here's a comment from Neil Cross, the creator and writer of the BBC detective series *Luther*:

> Creating a television show is all about chaos. It doesn't matter how diligent your planning might be, things change in the writing – new connections wait to be discovered and assimilated, accelerating stories in new, more exciting directions.

There are outlines, step-outlines and treatments to be written and re-written. There are producer's notes, director's notes, production notes. A million and one things can change; two million and five things actually do. A television show is alive, and it's hungry. I continue to submit my scripts in Final Draft. But all the work that gets done leading up to that submission – all the outlining, the brainstorming, the researching, the writing, the revising, the creation of structure from chaos – that gets done in Scrivener, the best writer's application in the world.

(Literature and Latte 2014)

While reading this we were reminded of the cognitive processes that underpin lesson planning (Savage 2014). In a similar way to how a screenwriter would want to keep track of characters, plots, sub-plots, locations and themes, the learning objectives and aims that are included within a lesson plan and that span across our units of work and curriculum maps can all be tagged and traced within the Scrivener environment.

As a teacher, you need to undertake a lot of writing. Although you will not be writing manuscripts of 80,000 words, you will be researching and writing significant pieces of text for the purposes of lesson planning. Scrivener provides an environment where your digital collections of materials from Evernote can be presented alongside a writing environment that allows you to connect and trace ideas through its innovative tagging mechanisms. While Scrivener is not free, it is definitely worth the small cost and we highly recommend it.

Practical task

Being to construct your own personal learning network using some of the above tools and any other tools that you have noted during your reading of this book. Spend some time acquainting yourself with how your chosen tools operate and personalising them to your own specific needs. Think about how the various tools you have chosen connect together and try and integrate them within the technology that you have available in a constructive way.

5 Visualising your personal learning network

Earlier in the chapter we mentioned visualisations of personal learning networks created by other teachers. We also considered the mapping of the London Underground by Harry Beck. We saw how important a graphical representation of a network was in allowing us to think differently about how things are connected together.

This book is about your relationship to your local environment. Throughout it, we have considered how the act and process of teaching in a school, and the curriculum that is offered to pupils through your work, can be enriched by an understanding of, and relationship with, your local area. Mapping out your own personal learning network is a powerful way to help you start to visualise these processes, understand how they relate to and inform each other, and think differently about them too.

Practical task

Prepare your own diagram of your personal learning network. Adopt whatever graphical approach you want but try to show the connections between the various elements of your network in some way. Why not share the result online via a blog post, a photograph on Twitter or a slide on a slide-sharing site?

Connectivism, pedagogy and personal learning networks

The competencies, behaviours and tools of a personal learning network can all help you develop your pedagogy as a teacher. The key is finding ways to challenge your existing practice and extend this through your network.

George Siemens and Stephen Downes have explored how we might re-fashion learning for the network society. By looking at networks and social learning in networks, they have developed a framework to understand what learning looks like in the twenty-first century. This framework was given the name 'connectivism' by Siemens in a paper published on his blog in 2005. In 'Connectivism: A learning theory for the digital age' he presents his theory by looking at theories of knowledge that pre-date our current Internet era:

> Objectivism (similar to behaviorism) states that reality is external and is objective, and knowledge is gained through experiences. Pragmatism (similar to cognitivism) states that reality is interpreted, and knowledge is negotiated through experience and thinking. Interpretivism (similar to constructivism) states that reality is internal, and knowledge is constructed.
>
> (Siemens 2005)

These traditions, he argues, tell us what learning is, and they have been very influential in shaping classroom pedagogy by providing different models of learning that teachers can understand and promote through their pedagogical processes. Although each of these traditions represents complex theories, Siemens points to weaknesses in their explanations of how learning works.

Behaviourism implies a theory of learning where learning is the creation of habitual responses in specific circumstance and in response to particular stimuli. This leads to the idea of operant conditioning where pupils are understood to learn because they are presented with rewards. But there is no explanation of how giving someone a reward stimulates learning. There is simply a move to define what the reward is and begin more exploration in that direction.

In cognitivism, learning is described as creating a change in a learner's mental processes (inner mental activities such as thinking, memory, knowing and problem-solving). Teachers employ strategies for learning that focus on developing students' internal cognitive structures through learning particular techniques, procedures and forms of organisation. Famously, the mind is described in cognitivism through the metaphor of the 'black box', internal and knowable only through external manifestations.

Constructivism emphasises that knowledge is something that can be created on the basis of current knowledge and experience. Students learn through the experience of discovery. This happens most effectively through hands-on, collaborative projects that focus on problem-solving and build new knowledge from what people already know (through 'scaffolding'). Exactly how the construction occurs is, however, mysterious and once again posited on the inner workings of the 'black box' of the mind.

Siemens suggests that common to these ways of thinking about knowledge is that 'learning occurs inside a person' (ibid.). What they do not include is the learning that takes place outside of people (institutional knowledge or knowledge stored in organisational repositories) or between people and actively constituted within social connections. As we have seen in this chapter, our understanding of the world is increasingly informed by our understanding of networks and more and more networks are informing our world. Siemens is suggesting that learning occurs when we embark on the process of connecting to and feeding information into a learning community such as that based within our school, our physical locality or the virtual worlds we inhabit. That community is a node on a network that connects to other nodes in order to share information. The process is cyclical. We connect to the network to share and find new information. Understanding is changed as a result and that result is once again shared with the community as we look to find new information. Learning is both knowledge consumption and creation. So, 'the capacity to form connections between sources of information, and thereby create useful information patterns, is required to learn in our knowledge economy' (ibid.).

What is important about connectivism is that it is less about technology and more about creating the conditions, spaces and opportunities for knowledge to be created. Those conditions, spaces and opportunities are found in people and the connections between them: in the networks that people create and nurture. These networks take many forms, but our suggestion in this book is that your local area is one vitally important one! It is also a central argument of this book that schools, and your work within a school, can facilitate these processes for your students.

Stephen Downes has taken many of these ideas and considered them in the context of the roles that teachers play in the educational process. Have you ever stopped to ask yourself what your role is as a teacher? How would you describe it to an imaginary guest at a party who has no knowledge about you and your work? Downes' recent research has identified multiple roles that a teacher could adopt. These are presented below in Table 7.1 together with a brief explanation summarised from his work (Downes 2013).

Reflective task

Consider the following key questions:

- What kind of teacher are you? Which of Downes' roles did you think best described your own work?
- Which ones describe the work of other teachers who have taught you, or whom you have perhaps seen teaching recently?
- How do you think the specific roles that Downes identifies could help you create a networked approach within your teaching?
- What are the consequences for our students and how they learn in respect to the specific teaching roles outlined in Table 7.1?

Table 7.1 Downes' teaching roles

Teacher roles	Explanation
The Learner	'As someone who models the act of learning, the teacher helps students with this most fundamental of skills. This includes getting exited about something new, exploring it, trying it out and experimenting, engaging with it and engaging with others learning about it.'
The Collector	'Teachers have always been collectors, from the days when they would bring stacks of old magazines into class to the modern era as they share links, resources, new faces and new names. They find materials related to their own interests, keep in tune with student interests. They are the maven, the librarian, the journalist or the archivist.'
The Curator	'The curator is one who organises and makes sense of that which has been found. The curator is like a caretaker and a preserver, but also a creator of meaning, guardian of knowledge, or an expert at knowing. A curator is a connoisseur, one who brings quality to the fore, one who sequences and presents.'
The Alchemist	'The alchemist mixes the ordinary and mundane into something new and unexpected. The alchemist practices the "mix" of remix, the "mash" of mash-up, the "collage" of bricolage. The alchemist sees patterns and symmetries in distinct materials and brings them together to bring that out.'
The Programmer	'The programmer builds sequences into machines, manipulates symbols to produce meaning, calculates, orders, assembles, and manages.'
The Salesperson	'The salesperson plays an important role in providing information, supporting belief and motivating action. The salesperson is the champion of a cause or an idea.'
The Convener	'The convenor is the person who brings people together. A convener is a network builder, a community organiser. Conveners are leaders, coaches, and administrators; they are collaboration builders, coalition builders, enablers or sometimes even just pied pipers.'
The Coordinator	'The coordinator organises the people or things that have been brought together for the common good. A coordinator is an eminently practical person, organising schedules, setting expectations, managing logistics, following up and solving problems. A coordinator is a connector and an integrator, but most of all, a systems person.'
The Designer	'The purpose of the designer is to create spaces for learning, whether they are in person, on paper or online. They attend to flow, perspectives, light, tone and shading.'
The Coach	'The coach does everything from creating synergy and chemistry in a group to providing the game plan for learning, raising the bar and encouraging players to higher performance. Though the coach is on the side of the learner, in the learner's corner urging them on and giving advice, the coach also serves a larger or higher objective, working to achieve team or organisational goals.'
The Agitator	'The agitator is the person who creates the itch a person's education will eventually scratch. The role of the agitator is to create the seed of doubt, the sense of wonder, the feeling of urgency, the cry of outrage. The agitator is sometimes the devil's advocate, sometimes the revolutionary, sometimes the disruptive agent, and sometimes just somebody who is thinking outside the box.'
The Facilitator	'The facilitator makes the learning space comfortable. Their role is to cove the process or the conversation forward, but within a broad range of parameters that will stress clarity, order, inclusiveness, and good judgment. The facilitator keeps things on track and within reason, gently nudging things forward, but without typically imposing his or her opinions or agenda onto the outcome.'

The Moderator	'The moderator governs and prunes. The moderator of a forum is concerned about decorum, good behaviour and rules. He or she will tell people to "shush" while the movie is playing, trim the trolls from the discussion thread, and gently suggest that the experienced pro ought to go more easily on the novice.'
The Critic	'The critic is the person who asks for evidence, verifies the facts, assesses the reasoning, and offers opinions. They are an aide to understanding, one who will extract the threads of a tangled presentation and make them clear. As logic texts everywhere proclaim, criticism consists first of exposition and only then of examination.'
The Lecturer	'The lecturer has the responsibility or organising larger bodies of work or thought into a comprehensible whole, employing the skills of rhetoric and exposition to make the complex clear for the listener or reader.'
The Demonstrator	'Demonstration has always been a part of education, whether a carpenter demonstrating proper mitering to an apprentice or a chemist demonstrating proper lab technique to a class. Traditionally, demonstration has been done in person, but today people who demonstrate can use actual equipment, simulations, or video to tell their stories.'
The Mentor	'The role of mentor is itself multi-faceted, ranging from sharp critic to enthusiastic coach, but outweighing these is the personal dimension, the presence of the entire personality rather than some domain or discipline. Not everyone can be a mentor, not every mentor can take on too many prodigies, and of all the roles described here, that of the mentor is most likely to be honorary or voluntary.'
The Connector	'The connector draws associations and makes inferences. The connector is the person who links distinct communities with one another, allowing ideas to flow from art to engineering, from database design to flower arranging. The connector sees things in common between disparate entities and draws that line between them, creating links and collaborations between otherwise isolated communities and disciplines. The connector sees emergent phenomena, patterns across different groups or different societies, or conversely, identifies the unusual, unique or unexpected.'
The Theoriser	'The theoriser tries to describe how or why something is the case. The theoriser often works through abstraction and generalisation, which leads to critics saying he or she is not very practical, but without the theoriser we would have no recourse to very useful unseen phenomena such as mass, gravity or information. The theoriser is also the person who leads us to develop world views, finds the underlying cause or meaning of things, or creates order out of what appears to be chaos.'
The Sharer	'The sharer shares material from one person to another on a systematic basis. The sharer might be the person making e-portfolios available, the person managing the class mailing list, or the person passing along links and reflections from outside. But ultimately, what the sharer offers most are cultures, concepts and ideas.'
The Evaluator	'The evaluator is more than a marker of tests and assigner of grades; the evaluator does not merely assess declarative knowledge or compositional ability, but instinct and reactions, sociability, habits and attitudes.'
The Bureaucrat	'The bureaucrat provides the statistics so much needed by the coordinator, manages the finances and resources, tracks the services needed by facilitators, organises accountability procedures and maintains systemic coherence.'

Source: Downes (2013).

It is probably the case for most of us that we will recognise a number of these roles within our personality and role as a teacher. However, like any taxonomy it does challenge us to think about our comfort zone and imagine things differently. What would it be like to be the 'teacher as agitator'? How could I develop my teaching so I bring more of the 'teacher as alchemist' to the fore? Questions such as these will help you think differently about your role within the classroom; this will begin to have a bearing on how to begin to plan particular teaching episodes and reimagine your role within them.

Downes' representation of teaching roles is one example of how we can use provocative ideas within our personal learning networks to inform our pedagogy as teachers. Many of his roles depend on us as teachers being able to engage with and relate to others. Surely we know, better than anyone else in our society, that teaching is built upon relationships with others. After all, we teach human beings not robots! Being reflective about our pedagogical role and challenging our thinking and acting in this arena through connecting with the ideas of others are vital skills in becoming an excellent teacher.

Summary

We began this chapter by considering small, area-based and social networks such as those found within Victorian mill towns and the present-day local market town. These are vital to our sense of who we are and how we relate to others. They are also central to our sense of identify, in a psychological sense, and well-being. We noted how networks can be simplified or made transparent through how they are mapped.

The concept of your own personal learning network is vitally important in today's society. The web has transform every area of our lives together in twenty-first century Western society. Teaching is not immune to these changes.

When we consider what we mean by 'local', it is useful to remember that this can mean very different things depending on the context in which we are working. If we use 'local' in a geographical sense, as we have done throughout most of this book, then an area-based curriculum approach will contain one set of pedagogical ideas and approaches; we have explored many examples of this in the various case studies included in the early chapters. If we consider what we mean by 'local' in a virtual sense, then this is a hugely expanded notion that depends on the networks that we choose to develop and live our 'virtual' lives within.

Which is more important or powerful, the 'geographical' local or the 'virtual' local? It is impossible to say. But what we can say is that it will not be either one or the other. It will be a blend of the two and the precise mix of one or the other will depend on a whole host of other factors and considerations. The key point of this chapter is that through engaging in the production of a personal learning network of your own in a systematic and serious way, you will be able to make informed and justifiable decisions about how you engage with your locality in whatever shape or form this presents itself.

In all of this it is important to remember that you, your subject, your school, your pupils are individuals. Although we clearly enjoy linking together, working as groups and having a sense of belonging, sometimes it is right to maintain one's privacy. Sometimes sharing and connecting is not appropriate for all kinds of reasons. As

Andrew Keen writes, 'our uniqueness as a species lies in our ability to stand apart from the crowd, to disentangle ourselves from society, to be let alone and to be able to think and act for ourselves' (Keen 2012: 193). Our curriculum in school must enable this. It must allow us to work in groups, to be social, but to have an individual voice too. There is a balance here, but only you and your local community will be able to tell where that is.

In all of this, lead by example. Build a personal learning network of your own and show your colleagues and your pupils what a powerful tool this can be in connecting you to the ideas of others, whether they are community group based on the estate next to the school or a social enterprise within a township in South Africa. In the next chapter we will turn our attention to the way in which you can work in a partnership with others to help develop a collaborative area-based curriculum approach. This chapter has been about you and your tools. We have focused on the development of your own personal learning network. We have considered the tools that this might contain, how you might use these and the kinds of behaviours that can help facilitate a productive environment through which you can engage with others within your school, local area and beyond. As you seek to do this, here are a few final words of advice.

First, work in the open. Teaching is too often characterised as a private activity, something that takes place behind the closed door of your classroom. While writing this chapter, we heard about one teacher who was complaining about her head teacher who used to make unannounced visits to her classroom. She found this threatening and difficult to cope with. While we can quite imagine a set of circumstances where this could be problematic, for the vast majority of teachers we would suggest that having a physical open door to your classroom is always beneficial. Welcome any visitor to your classroom – senior school leader, fellow teaching colleague, parent or student – and share your own and your students' work. Adopt the same principle with your online profile. The more public you make your work the more opportunities there will be for people to make connections with you, and the better and more productive your network will become.

Second, obtaining feedback on your network and the work that it helps you facilitate is vital. Develop a trusted, smaller group of friends who can give you honest input and feedback. We do this in our work, both in terms of our teaching in the university and in our writing (such as this book). We actively encourage open, constructive and critical feedback of our work from this trusted group of friends. The benefits are immense.

Finally, resist the urge to conform in terms of your thinking. Actively move out of your comfort zone on occasions. Engage with different perspectives and find people to disagree with (politely). Proverbs 27:17 tells us that 'as iron sharpens iron, so one person sharpens another'. In constructing your personal learning network, you are committing yourself to a process of self-improvement and pedagogical development. You are demonstrating a whole range of professional attributes that mark you out as a teacher who is serious about your work and wanting to develop yourself further. You will find like-minded teachers out there who want to do the same. You can help each other and spark off each other too. Enjoy the journey and who knows where it will take you.

References

Downes, S. (2013) 'The Role of the Educator'. www.huffingtonpost.com/stephen-downes/the-role-of-the-educator_b_790937.html [last accessed 2 October 2013].

Keen, A. (2012) *Digital Vertigo: How today's online social revolution is dividing, diminishing and disorienting us.* London, Constable and Robinson.

Literature and Latte (2014) 'Who Uses Scrivener?' www.literatureandlatte.com/whousesscrivener.php [last accessed 4 August 2014].

Savage, J. (2014) *Lesson Planning: Key concepts and skills for teachers.* London, Routledge.

Siemens, G. (2005) 'Connectivism: A learning theory for the digital age'. www.elearnspace.org/Articles/connectivism.htm [last accessed 14 April 2014].

Chapter 8

Developing teaching and learning partnerships

Introduction

While most of this book is focussed on helping you develop your pedagogy in new directions, we acknowledge that partnership approaches to the provision of new curricular arrangements in school are becoming more common. This has been a theme in many of the case studies used in previous chapters. In this chapter we will examine some examples drawn from the work of schools we have worked with across the north-west of England. We will reflect on these and ask some basic questions about the characteristics of effective partnerships and how these can be developed through local networks (and also extended through national and international networks).

Working in partnership is a key component of any area-based curriculum approach. These partnerships could involve other schools, local authority services, creative practitioners and local industry. But, more importantly, these partnerships will also mean rethinking how we work with parents, carers, pupils and others.

As we have noted in other chapters of this book, the idea of conceptualising your school as a lead partner in the local community is a key to developing an area-based curriculum. We have emphasised that schools cannot see themselves, or be seen, as autonomous to the community in which they 'serve'. It would be a mistake at this point though to see this as a one-way process where the school is there to just serve the local community. It could be argued that over time this could be more detrimental to the school and community than beneficial.

There is something more important and empowering that we must acknowledge in basing our curriculum on the assets and knowledge that are contained within our local area. The principle of partnership and an area-based curriculum must work towards the idea that the local area is a resource, that partners do not just add to what we already do, but rather that together we can enhance and reshape the way in which our locality is used to inform a curriculum. When done well, this can become a powerful and transforming agent of change in our pupils' lives.

Defining partnership

> Partnership working between schools has been a dominant feature of educational policy discourse for many years now both in the UK and internationally.
> (Higham and Yeomans 2009)

Partnership will not be a new word or idea to anyone who has worked in education over recent times. Indeed, there are many forms of partnership that we can see in schools today.

1 A partnership of educational organisations

In the United Kingdom, partnership working encompasses diverse models including initiative such as the Leading Edge Partnership Programme, the Specialist Schools and Academies model of schools working together around specialisms, and the development of cross-phase school partnerships to deliver wider programmes of work. Schools and universities work in partnership to deliver courses of initial teacher education as well as to provide access to higher-level academic qualifications.

2 A partnership for professional development

Many of the organisations listed above may have formed part of your own process of professional development. Your own journey towards teaching has also been characterised by various partnerships. You will have combined academic study with personal beliefs and professional training. This training will have taken in knowledge and skills along its way from key partners such as universities, schools where you have undertaken teaching placements and perhaps other organisations too such as subject associations or teaching unions. As you enter into school and work as a teacher, you become a partner in that school and bring to it your own personal skills and beliefs.

3 A partnership with pupils

It is the same too for the pupils that we teach. As Thomson (2002) argues, all pupils come to school with 'virtual schoolbags' of experiences, knowledge and resources developed in their lives outside school; but only some schools and teachers go on to draw upon their pupils' schoolbags in the construction of their curricula.

This key point is important for us to consider as we set out our thoughts on partnership for our curriculum. We need to consider carefully what parts of our 'schoolbags' are drawn upon and whether this agrees with the principles we set out for what is important in our curriculum. Can working in partnership help us promote a more diverse sharing of ideas and a wider understanding of what is important in any given local community?

4 A partnership with parents

Parents and carers are vital in this mix. They are key educators of the pupils we teach. In this most obvious of partnerships, we need to work hard to make sure that we work collaboratively. True partners do not work in opposing ways. Critically, the evidence from existing research and projects does not imply that parents should be tasked with taking on the role of formal educators; instead, the aim of such partnerships should be to work with parents to understand how they might bring their own distinctive expertise and resources to bear in the school setting. As such, the challenge is not to harness parents simply to the existing goals of the school, but to enable educators to understand and engage with the resources that exist outside the school, and to engage with parents in a debate about curriculum design and purposes.

This could be seen as a key shift in the way in which we approach all partners who may have a bearing upon our curriculum in school. It is important to acknowledge at the beginning of this chapter that all partnerships, whoever they are with, need to be judged against how they bring their own distinctive expertise and resources to bear in the school setting. At the heart of this relationship needs to be a shared understanding of what each partner can bring to this new curriculum. There needs to be a meaningful dialogue between the partners, which gives a shared vision of what being in 'partnership' means.

So, what we are imagining here, and seeking to promote throughout this chapter, is a change in the way you conceptualise partnership. In our experience, partnership work is often seen as a short project focused on a local figure or historical site, or a visit to school by an external music or drama group. Clearly, there is nothing wrong with these activities per se and they are one of the effective ways in which partners can work in school. We want to expand this definition of partnership, and place the school and the curriculum in a wider context within which the local area itself can become a strong formative influence.

Who are your local partners?

This is a vitally important first question. Have you ever stopped to consider who your local partners might be? In addition to the obvious groups that we have discussed already (pupils, parents, etc), there will be many other partners scattered across your local area that you could begin to think about working with. Establishing a database of partners is something that you, and your school, could begin to do very easily.

The benefits of such partnerships are many and varied. Throughout the case studies in this book, we have seen how partnerships can be constructed that benefit both partners equally. It is not about an external partner doing a favour for a school, or vice versa. Nor does it have to be purely a charitable exercise either. Ask any professional fundraiser! They will tell you that partnerships are crucial to the securing of funds for projects across all sectors.

Increasingly in education, we are beginning to recognise the importance of partnership work. So, where can you start?

1 Educational partners

These might be organisations in your area that are primarily there to support your work in school. In the past, these may have included area coordinators for subjects or curriculum support teams based within local authorities. More recently, these will now be organisations that have been privatised or partially centrally funded but also charged with a responsibility for supporting your school curriculum or national or local strategies. Included in this would be organisations such as music hubs or teaching schools within an alliance.

2 Business partners

Local businesses can become powerful partners for many reasons. You may already have a local business as a sponsor for your school, or perhaps individual subjects in school have their own links to businesses in related areas. However, the benefits of business partners are wide-ranging. Try and think beyond the obvious links and be creative about the potential partnerships that local businesses might offer.

3 Voluntary sector partners

In your local area you will have a vast number of voluntary organisations that have a small amount of full-time staff supplemented by volunteers. This may include local heritage centres, transport museums, communities of artists, reading groups and other literary associations, organisations that work in early years or end of life care, and many more. These are the sorts of organisations that are used to working in partnership. It is how they grow and survive. They are also the types of organisations that schools have traditionally used for visits and other work.

4 National organisations

Although not always local to your school, there are many national organisations that are supportive of the work done by schools and can help put you in touch with potential partners. These larger partners often find it difficult to find schools who are willing to work in partnership. They may offer 'calls' for partnership working via their websites or through particular projects that they are want to develop. Keeping in touch with larger organisations like this is worthwhile via their websites and, if possible, through making contact with their educational officer. Informal conversations and sharing information about your work with these organisations can often lead to exciting formal partnerships further down the road.

Reflective task

Make a list of prospective partners or local stakeholders who could have an investment in your school curriculum. Keeping your pupils at the centre of this thinking, imagine how you might bring together these parties to help design a curriculum project. At this stage keep ideas small and try not to create lots of extra work. Think more of how this input might make connections between existing units or schemes and the local area.

In the following part of the chapter we are going to consider two case studies that provide interesting examples of partnership working. They are quite distinct, coming from different sources and containing contrasting ways of working. As you read through them we would encourage you to take notes of ideas that you feel have made these examples successful. Keep in mind the previous task, though, and try and maintain a clear focus on the goals that you might want to achieve for your own curriculum project within an existing unit of work.

Partnership working in music education

When we taught in schools during the late 1990s and early 2000s, the local music service was the centralised service that provided visiting instrumental music teachers to our schools. They were centrally funded and provided free music lessons on various instruments. These peripatetic music teachers supported individual instrumental lessons and often ran the schools' extracurricular musical activities, supporting the music teacher. More recently, funding mechanisms changed and most schools began to 'buy in' peripatetic lessons for pupils who were also expected to cover some or all of the cost.

In 2012, music hubs were created. Some of these were new versions of single music services; in other areas, individual services came together to form larger hubs that serve multiple regions:

> Music Education hubs were formed to 'ensure that every child aged 5–18 has the opportunity to sing and learn a musical instrument, and to perform as part of an ensemble or choir.' They are there to help 'young people to take their talent further' and to support the pupils at every school to take part in local ensembles, partnerships with nationally funded music organisations, including National portfolio organisations or through involvement in the Music and Dance Scheme.
>
> (ACE 2012)

Partnership work is central to the operation of a music education hub:

> Hubs will be expected to form strong partnerships with local authorities, schools, music organisations, practitioners and communities to provide quality music education across the whole country – while delivering better value for money and greater accountability.
>
> (ACE 2012)

Music education hubs are also meant to present an alternative, more coherent, approach to music education that brings together the work done by visiting instrumental teachers with the curriculum-based musical activities within a school. Over time, the two had become quite distinct in many schools. Hubs are encouraging a different approach, one which places the pupil at the heart of the music education process. It is within this context that our first case study should be viewed.

Case Study 1 Crich School

> Today, music is central to the life of the school. As well as class-based music lessons, led by class teachers, the whole school has a weekly ensemble session – timetabled during the school day – where every child participates in mixed-age rehearsals of either orchestra, choir, or recorders.
>
> (Ofsted 2012)

Crich School is a small junior school in the heat of the Peak District. The school works within the Derbyshire City and County Music Partnership. This was formed as a joint venture between Derby City and Derbyshire County Council. The school has adopted a philosophy of 'every child a musician' (ibid.) with support from their musical partners. This is more than just offering lessons to pupils but is about adopting a philosophy of partnership work that embeds music within the curriculum.

Music at Crich School is inclusive; the activities are managed in a way 'that allows pupils of all ages and all abilities to work, learn, and make music together' (ibid.). 60 per cent of the pupils at the school play in the orchestra and the rest are members of the choir, the recorder group or both. Music is arranged to suit the abilities of all and to support activities and presentations in the school. This is supported by all of the staff including the teaching assistants.

Quality is the hallmark of this partnership approach, within which the head-teacher has a vital role in maintaining communication with the music service, ensuring that expectations and high standards are understood by all and implementing a robust quality assurance programme.

Additionally, the music service runs its own 'Quality Mark Initiative'. Through this, the music service can recognise and reward schools that are providing a quality musical experience for their pupils in partnership with themselves.

Some obvious and subtler ideas and lessons can be drawn from this successful work in music education within a primary school.

1 Strong management

It takes drive, initiative and persistence from at least one individual to develop a vision of how things in a school can change. In this case, the head teacher had a vision to change the school's music provision and worked with external partners to factilitate this. Beyond just facilitating music lessons for the pupils, which has been done in many schools for many years, the head teacher's vision really challenged and developed the school's ethos surrounding music education. The concept of 'every child a musician' was a vital one that informed the partnership provision from the beginning.

2 Key partners

The steps taken at the start were small, replicating pervious models, but the addition of an external partner really developed the provision within the school quickly. Prior to the collaboration with the music service, an enthusiastic and knowledgeable parent was responsible for starting a recorder ensemble within the school. What happened at that point was that the activity, the establishment of the musical ensemble, created something much larger than the sum of its parts. This drove a much larger change in the school that the head teacher was able to manage and promote with a larger external partner. This leads us on to the next point.

3 Curriculum change supported by partnership

Partnership work should not be seen as always trying to bring in something that is missing from the curriculum or focus on the areas where you may feel you pupils do not achieve. For many years, this deficit model characterised many curriculum projects that often failed to achieve much. The strength of the partnership in this case study began in a vision that saw music as an integral part of the curriculum itself, as a key driver in supporting and promoting the school's ethos and its wider achievement and also as a way of bringing the pupils together through musical activities.

The same principles and lessons could be applied to different curriculum or partnership areas. It was when a partnership philosophy became imbedded into the curriculum that the outcomes became much stronger. Although this came initially from the drive and focus of one teacher, it did not take long before the whole staff got behind the initiative.

This case study illustrates the importance of partnership work being conceived as a two-way process. Partners can only provide so much to your school, to your work or to your classroom. You have to consider how this work becomes embedded into the curriculum, be this as a whole philosophy or within a certain department's work or even individual projects. You then need to consider how the work you do with your pupils will feed back to the partner. What is in it for them? How does your work help to raise their standards, impact something new or facilitate new areas of work?

Partners are not always easy to find and the first steps into partnership are often quite daunting. There is an almost natural feeling of 'what do they want from us' or 'what will they pay us'. However, what can be seen from the next case study is that many local organisations and businesses of all kinds are looking for ways to develop, evolve and build through this kind of partnership working with schools. There is a slower revolution in which partners have something to learn from schools and their pupils, and the 'payment' they receive may be worth more than any potential monetary gain.

Reflective task

At this point, take time to edit any notes you have made about the case study.

- What are the key points to note which relate to your work, pupils or school?
- Are there any emerging themes or ways of working which would be easier to develop in your school?

Case Study 2 Dogsthorpe Junior School and Railworld

This case study is about partnership work between Dogsthorpe Junior School and Railworld. Railworld is a railway heritage site and centre for sustainable transport located on a split site spanning the River Nene near Peterborough city centre. Like many community partners, it is a small organisation with only two full-time members of staff who are supplemented by volunteers. Railworld has been in existence since 1985, but at the time of the case study it had recently opened an education centre and wanted to be known for 'more than just trains' (RSA 2012).

The partnership between the school and Railworld began as a happy coincidence rather than a planned curriculum or learning partnership. Gemma Brown, a teacher at the school, was looking for somewhere to display some cars that the pupils had created and she contacted John Turner, the manager at Railworld.

> The first conversation John and I ever had was 'I've got a load of cars that my wonderful learners have built; I need somewhere to display them'. John said 'oh, you can display them at mine', and that was literally where we started.'
>
> (Ibid.)

> After this, John visited the school and, with support from the RSA, the project was created. It turned into a one-year embedded curriculum project that allowed pupils to cover National Curriculum content 'through a real life project' (ibid.). Through it, Year 5 children helped to rebrand Railworld from the 'railway museum' image of its past into a 'sustainable transport centre' for the future (RSA 2012). Activities were planned so that children visited the site and Railworld employees came into school. Teachers took responsibility to ensure that activities such as numeracy, literacy and geography were embedded suitably into the curriculum.
>
> Additional spin-offs from this project included the school being invited to take part in other civic redevelopment projects. Year 5 pupils were invited to the local town hall for a conference discussing 'matters affecting Peterborough' (ibid.) They were told that they were being brought to meet the Mayor, council officials and local councillors to give their input into a range of local decision-making processes.

Working with partners is more then just developing a link to new skills outside of the classroom. One of the key themes of this book is that by looking around what people and history you have in your local area, you can give better understanding to your curriculum and more closely link it to your pupils. This partnership was clearly successful and beneficial to all involved, but what lessons can we draw from this partnership work which are common to the previous study and what breaks new ground?

I Looking at the partnership from the school's perspective

Dogsthorpe School has a broad mix of pupils, many of whom have English as an additional language. The head teacher at the time of the project clearly saw that the school was more than just another slightly invisible junior school in the middle of a 'post-war council estate' (ibid.). She analysed the changing diversity of the school and saw engagement with the school's local area as an opportunity to make a connection between the school, its pupils and the parents in the community.

On the estate were people and families who had helped create the neighborhood, builders and skilled tradesman who had invested part (if not all) of their lives in this area. Juxtaposed against this were newly arrived families, who were seeking to establish new roots in the area. The head teacher realised there was an opportunity to help this diverse community through an area-based curriculum approach:

> Our school site is set in the heart of a massive post-second world war show-case housing estate representing the nation's attempt to rebuild a better future for the surviving families of the war: the builders of the estate still live amongst us, some struggling to come to terms with the change in identity of their locality ... we will not know what our community knows, cherishes and aspires to unless we engage with it in a way that we have not done so up to know.
>
> (Oftsed 2012)

So a new 'curriculum' that connected to this would benefit all. She also saw that many of their curriculum ideas were becoming outdated and lacked a connection to the pupils at the school. She wanted to break the stereotypes of schools in the area and make the pupils and parents realise that this was their school and it was about serving their needs.

2 Looking at the partnership from Railword's perspective

Railworld knew that they had more to offer to a partnership than just visits and looking at trains, but they were not sure what this was. They had good links to local heritage and environmental sectors in the city but were keen to develop a curriculum or school connection.

The school also happened upon a partner who was not set up to provide a service to the school. The chance interaction between a teacher and a regular member of staff at Railworld began this journey for them.

The school took a chance to get the pupils outside of the classroom on more than just educational visits. There was an opportunity for the pupils to engage with global issues of sustainable transport and impact on the environment. This could then be linked to issues that were relevant in Peterborough about town planning, transport links and the rail centre. This then further enabled them to place these lessons within their own school and community and see how this impacted their daily lives.

This chance interaction which started this partnership definitely has a sense of some luck to it as Railworld were looking for a partner to develop new work and the school teacher wanted a place to display the pupils' work. Railworld and Dogsthorpe School both established what they wanted from the project with support from RSA guidelines. This gave a clear starting point from which the partnership could develop. It also made it clear to both partners how the work would be mutually beneficial.

3 Building the partnership

The teachers and Railworld staff met to exchange skills and to support each other, which gave them a firm base for their professional relationships rooted in each others' complementary and diverse skills. It was important for each party to understand the other's organisation at the outset.

This then enabled them to meet and discuss a shared vision for how both partners can benefit from being in partnership. It was beneficial that the school was looking outside of its own area and skills to develop new ideas that would enthuse the teachers but also take account of government directives. Railworld was looking for the input of children, a new critical eye that would develop what they had to offer. Key to this, with the support of the RSA, was to keep the pupils at the centre of this, making their educational journey the driving force behind this work.

This initial formal agreement was important. It gave the main outline of the project so that work throughout the year could be more flexible. Neither party would have wanted to commit in minute detail for a year's work, but a clear framework for the project would help the establishment of a productive partnership.

Friendships and professional relationships grew from this that were reflected in interviews with the teachers:

He respects my side of it and I respect his ... I did do some work for him to deliver to his trustees and all sorts ... so we did the professional side first and because that all worked and we did get on, it's now meant that we are a lot more flexible as partners, really. I can now text him and say 'are you available tomorrow afternoon to come into school?'

(Ofsted 2012)

4 Developing the project

These initial aims were well focused and not overly ambitious in planning. They also could be embedded into any part of the school curriculum as a single project or more long-term into an educational philosophy. The 'projects are embedded within the core curriculum of the school, and can both enhance and challenge the National Curriculum' (ibid.).

Railworld had a simpler task for the pupils, to help with signage and rebranding, but behind this, using their involvements with more local and national organisations, the pupils were able to see the bigger picture.

i The goals (learning objectives)

There were several learning objectives that were present in the project. The partnership started with planning what the pupils and Railworld would do, the tasks, from this could then be developed the proposed learning. Initially, the head teacher wanted the school to be more connected to its local area and for parents within the community to know more about the school and have a sense that they were involved. It was also about the parents and pupils understanding how their local area was changing and how they are part of this change: as the teacher Gemma Brown put it, 'what Peterborough is, how it's changed, and how it's going to change, and our children's part within that' (Ofsted 2012). This more ambitious learning objective, which came through the project, was facilitated well by not making it the main aim of the activities or focus for the partnership. This was an outcome of the work that the pupils could do over the year.

ii Planning activities

The pupils took part in a range of activities throughout the year, but the first activity, 'a conference for all 90 Year 5 children at the Town Hall in September' (ibid.), was probably most key. This set the project up as important. The impact on the pupils would have been marked by how this was organised, who attended and how they were treated less as pupils and more as conference delegates. This activity was set up in school prior to the conference by looking at the issues that would be covered and giving the pupils some understanding of wider impact that travel and environmental concerns have.

From this, the conference organisers were able to plan lots of different sorts of activities. Pupils could be taken into workshops on separate issues, work with different people from the separate parts of the organisations or be supported in more individual or group tasks:

A heritage officer present said 'they gave great comments to us that really challenged how we present heritage (feel free to quote me!) to our stake-holders. The kids liked new buildings as they thought old ones were dirty, an interesting idea!'.

(Ibid.)

Later in the term and throughout the year the pupils visited Railworld and completed different activities. This included an input into how the centre could rebrand itself. The pupils were encouraged to give honest feedback, with suggestions for development in the future and how they could be encouraged to visit with friends and family.

These series of visits helped in developing the partnership relationships and enabled teachers and Railworld staff to communicate and plan. A final visit was made in the summer term so that pupils could see the very real impact of their work, how the nature reserve had been developed and how the new signage looked.

5 Using partnership to shape future curriculum

A very important aspect here is how through this work the school happened upon a 'realism' to the curriculum that can help shape the future of curriculum development in the school. All too often in education, pupils are asked to work for what can feel like 'work's sake'. As educators we know that this is not true, but to pupils in school developing learning and understanding takes time. Facts and figures, the 'knowing' of the curriculum can be easily measured and perhaps even favoured by some (but we won't go into that here). In our experiences with pupils, though, they can find challenges in how they learn, why they need to learn it and why it has relevance. All of these points, we hope, are tackled somewhere in this book.

The teachers and pupils made a discovery through this partnership work. They found that because the experiences related what they were learning, how they were learning and its context very much more closely, it had a greater relevance. It was not pretending to organise an event that wasn't happening, you weren't composing for a fictitious event, you weren't writing prose for a play that will never happen.

> I don't plan anything without a real audience and a real outcome and some ... impact on, you know the community or their lives.... We now plan our writing so it has proper purpose and audience ... nothing is done for the sake of it anymore.
>
> (RSA 2012)

6 Using partnership to 'break new ground'

> The whole point of this project is not a transactional agreement where you are taking someone's services to better your curriculum. You have got to be offering something back to those people ... John at Railworld is very, very keen for us to be part of the development of his museum, and he trusts us, and he values us, and he values the children's involvement.
>
> (Ofsted 2012)

In the first case study the music partnership provided much to the school but the impact was not as great in reverse. Of course there is a knock-on effect in employing services from the area, and the teachers will learn and develop. Here, though, the partnership was about contextualising the learning, bring the world into the classroom and the pupils' classroom into the wider world. It was about the school looking beyond its own walls to enrich the curriculum but also realising that over time this could help the community understand the school better. It would benefit all involved with the school. Key was that the partnership benefited both parties equally.

This work also enabled the school to re-frame the curriculum and build in new ideas. The school noted three clear differences for them in this way of working:

- Having professional conversations before a visit was planned about what the children would be doing in school before they get there, what they would follow up on, and whether they could then work in partnerships to build a bigger outcome over time;
- A genuine collaboration with shared goals for school and partner;
- Authentic outcomes for pupils, so that they can see their work having an impact on the real world.

(Ofsted 2012)

7 The impact of partnership work

i On the pupils

The data from the school shows that the pupils were clearly engaged by the project. As will be true for the teachers involved, we think there are two main factors for this:

TAKING WORK INTO THE REAL WORLD AND THE REAL WORLD INTO WORK

We don't want to repeat or labour this point but we would encourage you to think how you can use partnership to make the work that your pupils complete be more relevant to who they are, where they live and the wider world.

INVOLVING OTHERS IN PUPILS' EDUCATION

Pupils presume that teachers are just that, teachers, not real people with greater experiences. The positive impact of involving partners who support, lead, plan or just facilitate work within or outside of our schools should not be underestimated.

For the school here one of the main goals was to raise overall engagement with the school and curriculum, especially focusing on pupils who displayed signs of being less engaged. Meetings between teachers and parents provided anecdotal evidence that pupils were excited by the work they produced in this project and they took pride in keeping this at home. Attendance data reflected that there was an improvement linked to the partnership work and this is correlated with school visits by partners.

ii On teachers

The teachers were clearly very positive about the idea of the work and were happy to be supportive. They knew they were the curriculum experts and could easily bring learning objectives, outcomes and all the necessary 'curriculum parts' to the project. It was important that they didn't feel threatened by this work as though the partner would impose the requirements on them. The teachers quickly realised that all of their goals linked to the present national curriculum work could be embedded into a project such as this and the pupils wouldn't even notice. With time and reflection they will be able to do this even more successfully and consider the impact on the future curriculum for the school, keeping the pupils at the centre of this.

The teachers have also begun to be influenced, by the very nature of curriculum design, to develop their own ideas and practices. A key theme of this book would be that there cannot be a separation between curriculum development and teacher development. Although not a CPD session that can easily be delivered at school, linked to a relevant outcome measured easily in pupil progress over 20 minutes, this is key in all of this work.

Over time the teachers will reflect on how this has developed their professional skills and enabled them to re-engage with their own professional development and will consider new ways in which different vehicles can be used for the 'transport' of the curriculum.

Teachers as curriculum designers cannot know all there is to know. In a profession that asks us to be reflective practitioners, it can be easy to be blinded into thinking that everything must come from us. We are the professionals in the business of school, we are trained to teach and part of that training is deciding what to teach. The shift of paradigm reflected above does not need any of this to be less true, though. It is obvious that the teachers were still key in the success of this project. They are still key in using their professional skills to design and deliver the pedagogy that supports it.

Teachers involved with the project have learned a great deal about the barriers and rewards of working in partnership with other stakeholders. They report having developed specific skills in relation to risk assessment. They have also learned a great deal about Peterborough:

> Personally I've learnt loads about Peterborough! I now know who does what … I'm a lot more knowledgeable about … the council side of things … who's in charge of what, what the priorities for the city are, and once you know those, your curriculum can be built round those brilliantly.
>
> (Ofsted 2012)

iii Impact on the wider school

The school has embraced the idea of partnership and are looking to how each year group can have a partner to enhance the curriculum delivery. They have used this work as a chance for the community to know that this is their school and the school wants them to be involved. They have started with obvious links such as parent partners and are searching for new ideas.

Think how this could be started in your school. How can you attract the other teachers first? What is the hook for them? How can you then encourage them to want to make wider links and offer contacts that they know?

At Dogsthorpe School a simple notice board is collecting ideas but this is in the wake of this initial project. You will need to consider how this can be started for you, your pupils and your school and why people should want to be involved.

What could we learn from the case studies?

Curriculum

The national curriculum can be covered and enhanced by engagement outside of the classroom. This might be in extracurricular activities, visits or projects but is more about making the curriculum accessible, engaging and alive. Further themes to run through these concepts can be easily developed.

Partnerships

Start small, have a vision or meeting and build from here. You will need to be willing to break down barriers, find funding or find a way around what seem like barriers.

When you look, you will find more resources around your local area and school than you might think. The more you get involved with partners the more visible these will become.

Teachers

Teachers learn as much through working in partnership as the pupils do. It is about setting out on the path of discovery with a goal but learning from the journey. As with all work in school we often focus on the product or outcome, for obvious reasons, but the process will be key. There are many benefits in the teachers knowing more about the local area, its history and its resources so that they can better prepare the pupils they teach for the world they will be entering.

Reflection

Collect all forms of data in the project from curriculum work or meetings. Use this to interrogate and improve practice. Set up systems for this reflection to include your partners and feedback into the cycle of work.

Be honest about standards expected and set everyone up to succeed. Think about what you want to evaluate, why and whom that evaluation is for. Are you observing practice to improve delivery or quality or trying to collect some form of data to support progression? Different forms of assessment are needed and this needs to be considered. Try to build in mechanisms to measure attainment and progression. These are not the same thing and do not take a linear path in improvement.

Introducing ideas of partnership into your curriculum

There is no simple way of introducing these ideas and principles. The evidence around us suggests that it is not a simple journey and that it will take perseverance and some tenacity to take ideas forward. Setting this into a school world that has a busy-ness culture is not going to be easy. Contrary to some popular belief, teachers do not have lots of free time and long holidays to do very little. Drawing from the ideas of the RSA (2012), we could start with these key principles.

1   Look first close to school, to partners who could provide skills, opportunities or input to develop new curriculum ideas.
2   Look to partners who could benefit from the input of expertise found in your school, both from individuals and collectively.
3   Use the resources in school. Ask the pupils and connect to parents; do not feel that it is only the teachers who must drive this.
4   Look to focus on pupils in school and partners around school who are least engaged with the curriculum. If you can bring these on board, give new voice to those who are less represented in the formal education sector, others should be much easier to engage.
5   Be willing to engage with and solve potential barriers to the work. Be these logistical, monetary or time-based, those involved must be willing to acknowledge that these barriers will exist and they must be willing to work to solve them.
6   A mutual respect for all involved must be held. This needs to be linked to key times to assess the work, evaluate action and re-plan for future work. By instigating this at the project start you will alleviate the pressure to strive to a set goal of performance or to measure the project by just simple A to B outcomes. A willingness to be creative and try new ideas will benefit this.

The engagement with partners can uniquely develop your school curriculum. In so many ways schools can be convinced to stick to the same ideas. The 'one size fits all' approaches (RSA 2012) can sanitise schools. The 'parachuting in of universally applied "expertise" in the form of consultants, advisors and initiatives; and a universal set of targets that define the purpose and role of education at a national level' (ibid.) can seek to treat all schools the same and then make visible only the problems that you might encounter. Your school partners will be unique; even in areas that seem to have less obvious business, cultural or community partners they will exist. In fact, the more you have to 'dig' to discover these partners the more important the partnership may end up being – not just to your school but also to the partner or partners you are engaging with.

Conclusions

> Although progress has been made in some areas, many schools still feel compelled to provide a generic curriculum which fails to engage or enthuse young people, and that misses opportunities to draw on local resources to support young people's learning.
>
> (RSA 2010)

Working in partnership, in your local area, is going to be key to bring together all the other separate 'elements' raised in the other chapters of this book into a real and vibrant curriculum for your school. Although there has been a relaxing of what feels like centralised government curriculum control, we as teachers feel compelled still to look for direction from this. Much of this comes from how we will be assessed or judged as we are charged with the responsibility of drawing this together. Through this chapter we hope that you have begun to make a plan for how the inclusion of partners might still 'tick the educational boxes' but also enrich the curriculum for our pupils.

More importantly it can reset the deficit model that can be created by not reacting to the context of your school. National systems can seek to treat schools and pupils without the local context, to fit them to measurable norms and systems. Unless the context is seen as problematic it is often completely ignored. As teachers we know the importance of context in all we do, but do not neglect the wider context of your school community.

There is no simple solution to this, nor is one offered here. It is important that we see the possible disengagement of our school with our local area as a chance to make a difference: to analyse from the best possible point a real or perceived problem and do something to change this. Schools, teachers and their pupils are best placed to make sure that they are able to react to the community as much as act upon it.

The development of partnership should not just be left to those who perceive that their school is failing its community, though, whether failing academically or against any other internal or external measure. The successes inherent in all of this work should be enough to convince any curriculum designer to take on its relevance and importance for a journey most importantly of discovery. It is clear that partnership starts with shared goals, but what can be discovered on the journey can be even richer.

Engaging with partners will also help you to break a much-perceived model that area-based work has long been associated with trying to solve problems that are inherent in an area rather than trying to use the area to develop:

> Researchers in the field of education have long argued that area-based initiatives in education have come to be associated with a deficit view of communities and a psychological account of educational failure (passed down between families) rather than a structural critique of socio-economic factors leading to disadvantage.
>
> (RSA 2012)

It will be clear in your school that 'Children from some better off areas and communities are equipped to use the education system and meet its requirements more effectively than others' (ibid.), but this is a national perspective. You have a chance to work locally, to break the stereotypes and generalisations and use this as a way of changing for the positive, no matter what your starting point.

It is important to realise that if the school is going to be a catalyst for change in your area, a role often assigned to it without prior consultation, it will not do this in any type of isolation:

> The benefits of a more meaningful engagement between schools and their places of location are not one-way. Communities and the individuals within them also benefit from participation in civic life ... The social mixing and mutual learning generated via a wider network of people getting involved in the life of the school, building relationships, and working together toward common goals, may also increase levels of social capital, and promote community resilience to a range of actual and potential contemporary socio-economic changes and challenges. Schools provide a unique space for this collective activity to take place.
>
> (Ibid.)

There are other challenges that are inherent to all of the points that have been raised here, though. Discussions around changing the curriculum, who is involved with it and who will deliver it will being up new challenges in modern education. The RSA (2012) perceive these as:

1   The increasingly restrictive regulation of access of adults to children;
2   A perceived threat to the professionalism of the teacher;
3   How to ensure that decisions about curriculum are representative and include groups not usually engaged or represented in such processes;
4   How to ensure that local individuals and organisations, particularly poor families, are not simply 'commandeered' by schools in the service of the dominant national agenda;
5   How to ensure that young people's needs remain central.

You can read more extensively about this, but some issues will be more easily solved than others. Winning over some of the teachers in your school may take some time. Anyone who has worked in schools will know that growing focus on performance and the shift to standards-based teacher training have been seen by some as 'an unacceptable attack on teacher autonomy and teacher creativity, transforming teachers from professionals to technicians' (Whitty 2006, p. 12, cited in RSA 2012).

'Hence the proposition of a curriculum that is owned in partnership with a range of non-teacher stakeholders might be seen as one that threatens teachers' professional identity and autonomy' (RAS 2012). We believe, as other do, that this is not a truism. The teachers involved in case studies and other who have engaged with the process have not found this even when there may have been some initial worries.

One of the greatest strengths to come from partnership work can be to make the curriculum in school more real for the pupils. By this we mean that the pupils see a direct relevance in their work, how it connects both to them and the wider world. This can have several benefits.

Partnership work can also have a positive influence on the review of exciting schemes of work and of the curriculum and how they are delivered. Working in partnership is not about creating or adding to workload, giving the teachers and pupils more to do. It is about shifting the paradigms of how work can be planned, delivered, completed and evaluated. One of the greatest benefits can be in how teaching and learning in all the school's work can be influenced by the involvement in a partnership project.

This also links to our book's key theme that curriculum development is about teacher development. All too often we meet teachers in schools who have become bored and disengaged by their own continually changing curricula. That may be because even though the content may change, the assessment change and the rigours of checks increase, how they teach has not changed. It may use new technologies, but in old ways. How many interactive whiteboards do you see used as electronic blackboards?

The only constant that we have is change. Teachers embrace this as a profession as well as any, we believe. But with that constant change can come apathy and a tendency to stay the same. If you stay still for long enough the change will come back to you. Engagement with new partnerships can be an excellent way to learn ideas about yourself as a teacher and to develop new approaches. The constant enthusiasm for your work, passion to develop 'the new' and constant search for something 'better' will, we would argue, keep teaching and curriculum always fresh.

As a profession we are lucky to work with some of the most creative minds in society – children. It is only the imposition of rules, expectations and routines that stifles this creative curiosity. It is therefore important that we seek wherever possible to take away the imposition of assessments, rules and regulations to allow our curriculum to 'live'. The most important paradigm shift is just in the mathematical equation that is applied to the curriculum. We must make sure that we do not put the answers at the start and make a curriculum that matches. There clearly are parameters and guidelines that we have to work between but there are so many ways to do this. We must ensure that the answer comes at the end of the sum. There is always a multitude of ways to get to the same destination.

References

ACE (Arts Council England) (2012) 'Music Education Hubs'. www.artscouncil.org.uk/funding/apply-funding/funding-programmes/music-education-hubs/ [last accessed 20 June 2014].

Facer, K. (2010) *Towards an Area-based Curriculum: Insights and directions from the research*. www.thersa.org/__data/assets/pdf_file/0009/286983/116821106-Manchester-Curriculum-Report-FINAL.pdf [last accessed 14 July 2014].

Higham, J. and Yeomans, D. (2009) 'Working Together? Partnership approaches to 14–19 education in England, British Educational Research Journal' 36, pp. 1–23.

National Partnership Group (2012) 'Teaching Scotland's Future'. www.scotland.gov.uk/Publications/2012 November 207834 [last accessed 20 June 2014].

Ofsted (Office for Standards in Education, Children's Services and Skills) (2012) 'Music in Schools: Sound partnerships'. www.ofsted.gov.uk/resources/music-schools-sound-partnerships [last accessed 20 June 2014].

RSA (Royal Society for the encouragement of Arts, Manufactures and Commerce) (2009) *Manchester Curriculum, A Report and Reflections for Further Development*. London, RSA. www.thersa.org/action-research-centre/learning,-cognition-and-creativity/education/practical-projects/area-based-curriculum/reports-and-case-studies/manchester-curriculum-a-report-and-reflections-for-further-development [last accessed 15 July 2014].

RSA (2012) *Dogthorpe Junior School and Railworld*. www.thersa.org/__data/assets/pdf_file/0019/1000765/Dogsthorpe-Junior-School.pdf [last accessed 1 July 2014].

Thomson, P. (2002) *Schooling the Rustbelt Kids: Making the difference in changing times*, Sydney, Allen and Unwin UK, Trentham Books.

Chapter 9

Evaluating and sharing your work

Introduction

Congratulations on getting to the final chapter of our book on using your local area as a stimulus for curriculum development! We hope you have enjoyed the book so far and found it interesting, challenging and helpful. In this chapter, we are going to introduce a simple model that will help you take some of the ideas of this book and develop them within your own curriculum development activities. Following this, we will conclude our book with some further brief reflections on how the key lessons here can be sustained and developed in your work.

Introducing educational evaluation

Evaluation is an essential part of the curriculum development process. But it is important to state from the outset that we are not equating educational evaluation with educational assessment, and neither is it the same as reflection (or self-reflection). We will return to these point later in the chapter when we will explore how several key processes of assessment and reflection can help you with the process of educational evaluation.

Throughout this book, we have promoted the view that you, the teacher, are the central location or site of curriculum development. We are sure that some of you might have found this a surprising assertion. After all, it is common to think about the 'curriculum' as being out there, written by an examination board or the government and 'imposed' on your work as teacher. This is diametrically opposed to our view. In our opening chapter, we drew on Lawrence Stenhouse's mantra of 'no curriculum development without teacher development' to justify our key point that curriculum development starts with the individual teacher, their passion, knowledge **and location,** before informing pedagogy and branching out into collaborations with others. To reinforce this key point, we are going to draw on two key quotations from other writings by this influential thinker and advocate for teachers. In the following quotations, we find Stenhouse emphasising that teachers' work is worthy of detailed study. But not only that, it is worthy of study by teachers themselves! To this end, Stenhouse equates systematic enquiry into teachers and teaching to a form of educational research, especially when it involves teachers being constructively self-critical of their practice:

> It is not enough that teachers' work should be studied; they need to study it themselves.
>
> (Stenhouse 1975, 143)

Enquiry counts as research to the extent that it is systematic, but even more to the extent that it can claim to be conscientiously self-critical.

(Stenhouse 1985, p. 15)

If you have completed a course of initial teacher training recently, you will, no doubt, remember the process of evaluating your lesson. This is part of a tripartite process of planning, teaching and evaluation that many processes of initial teacher education are built around. Evaluation is integral to the process of learning to become a teacher. For us, like Stenhouse, that process of evaluating the curriculum that we are offering to our pupils is something that is embedded within the day-to-day work of a skillful teacher. In what follows, we are principally going to talk about a one-off evaluation designed for the purposes of evaluating a new area-based curriculum unit. But the skills that educational evaluation entails are intricately linked to the general skills required to be an effective teacher. For that reason, evaluation (in either a general or specific sense) is something that you will quickly become good at if you practice it regularly!

Education is a complex activity. Teachers know this better than anyone else. Watching education in action within a classroom or other learning environment is fascinating. What would a systematic enquiry into the teaching and learning that takes place in your classroom look like? What would it involve? And how might it relate to a process of curriculum development? These are some of the key questions that this chapter will consider.

Reflective task

Before reading ahead any further, take a moment to pause. What are the first few things that come into your head when you hear the word 'evaluation'? What do you consider to be the differences between evaluation, assessment and reflection?

What can educational evaluation help me achieve in my classroom?

Educational evaluation can help you understand more fully the activities that go on within your classroom. Like Stenhouse's view of educational research, evaluation is a tool that you can use to investigate your own practice in a systematic and self-critical way. It can also be an approach that teams of educators could employ to investigate specific pieces of curriculum development (i.e. a broader approach to using an area-based curriculum within your department or school).

For the purposes of this book, one of the key benefits of adopting a process of educational evaluation within your work will be to allow you to ascertain the value of a new piece of area-based curriculum development that you have implemented within your teaching. This will help inform your judgement about whether to run the unit of work again, how to improve on it, or how to take lessons from it and implement them into another area-based piece of curriculum development at a future date.

Evaluation involves many things and activities. As we have mentioned already, it is a very practical activity that sits well within your portfolio of work as a teacher. It includes looking at things, asking questions, listening to others, describing events and making interpretations. It is a skilful activity. Some people talk about it as an art form. But there are some important things to consider before adopting an evaluative approach in your classroom.

1 Evaluation can be dangerous! It is about making things that are often private more public

Despite significant shifts in the ways that our schools are organised and managed, teaching is often quite a private activity, done alone or perhaps with one other adult. Processes of evaluation will often challenge this privacy (but in a helpful way). As an example, how often is your work as a teacher opened up and shared with other teachers in your school? Perhaps you are observed as part of the performance management and appraisal systems in your school, but how often is it possible for other colleagues to watch you teach? How would you feel about it if they did? And how often do you see others teach within your school? Opening up what could be the private space of our classrooms to others might be one part of an evaluation methodology. How would you feel about this? When thinking about using evaluation as an educational tool, it is vital to consider the conditions under which it is carried out and to ensure that it maintains respect for people and their privacy. This makes conversations about the type of evaluation you want to undertake particularly important, especially if this is something that you are going to do with a team of people.

2 Evaluation is mainly about people

Building on the above, evaluation is not solely about educational programmes and initiatives, although one of its purposes can be (and will be in our chapter) to make judgements about them. Evaluation has a legitimate role to play in justifying new ventures, but it is important to reflect on and prioritise the roles that people play within these. So, in evaluation, as in curriculum development, people are central. In an educational setting, this would include teachers, pupils and other adults working within the school setting. When done well, evaluation can capture the life experiences of people within educational projects and use these to usefully explain the decisions you have made, or help you make better decisions in terms of your future curriculum development. Evaluation needs to be contextualised within peoples' lives.

3 Evaluation is not all about people

In the previous point we considered how evaluation could start with a consideration of the people within a project. But it is very important to recognise that it extends from them into all kinds of other contexts. Educational projects are not always what teachers or pupils who have participated within them might think or say about them. Educational projects are complicated sets of aspirations, values and experiences within which individuals' biographies, political values, contextual influences and much more beside conflict. This can cause difficulties for people on occasion. In the specific case of evaluating an area-based piece of curriculum development, an evaluation would want to consider a much broader array of local partners, organisations and culture than a traditional piece of evaluation centered on a standard piece of curriculum development. This makes it a very complex web of interaction that needs to be handled sensitively. Evaluation, when done properly, is helpfully challenging but supportive.

4 Evaluation has a formative and summative dimension

As we mentioned above, evaluation does have several points of contact with educational assessment. One of these similarities is that it has both a formative and summative role. One popular application of evaluation is to look at the specific aims and objectives of a piece of curriculum development and measure them against its outcomes or achievements (and these might have been studied through a particular method of assessment). This is seldom, if ever, a straightforward judgement to make. The wider the scope of an area-based curriculum development approach, the more its evaluation needs to have a subtle approach to measuring success or failure. A narrowly focused view on a curriculum's objectives would often fail to recognise the broader effects that the pupils who had studied that curriculum might have obtained. So, it is important to note that evaluation is often about keeping open educational opportunities rather that seeking to close them down prematurely. Formative approaches to evaluation emphasise this; summative evaluative comments need to be handled with care.

5 Evaluation will not find the truth about a specific piece of curriculum development

Although the notion of truth is attractive to us as educators, a more pragmatic approach to evaluation acknowledges that 'truth' is always difficult to establish within a complex set of circumstances such as those that exist within your classroom. This is not to say that evaluation should not be truthful in its application. In fact, having an ethical approach to the collection of evaluative data and the processes by which judgements are made about that data is essential. But in terms of outcomes, there is unlikely to be one 'truth' that the evaluation process will uncover. While your chosen assessment methods will enable you to examine the impact of a curriculum on your pupils' learning, our assertion here is that a focus on educational evaluation will enable your to reflect more deeply on the process of curriculum development within which, as our book's first key principle asserts, you are an integral part.

Designing an evaluation for an area-based curriculum

Having considered a number of important operating principles for educational evaluation, we will now turn our attention to how you can design an evaluation for an area-based curriculum development project. Although this curriculum development project might be a fictitious entity in your mind at the moment, the issues outlined below will be equally applicable whether the work is centered within your own teaching practice or is situated as part of a wider, collaborative project with other members of staff in your department or school.

Practical task

Choose a unit of work that you are going to be teaching in the following few months that has an area-based curriculum theme. As a one-off activity, use the advice below about educational evaluation to conduct an evaluation of your curriculum development unit. Working collaboratively with another colleague in your school would make this an even more meaningful activity. You would not necessarily need to agree on all the fine detail of the planned curriculum, but rather you could use your colleague as another source of inspiration and ideas, eyes and ears and, where possible, get them to visit your classroom to assist in providing feedback to you about teaching during this unit of work. Perhaps you could return the favour if they were to do a similar study of their own? See if you can forge such a relationship with a colleague.

1 Right at the outset, commit to being a creative and reflective teacher

As with all aspects of teaching and learning, creativity and an ability to be reflective are key hallmarks of effective curriculum development and educational evaluation. Designing an area-based curriculum and an accompanying evaluation might seem like a rather dry exercise in planning and preparation. It shouldn't be! In both, you will want to build in opportunities for creativity (on your part as the teacher and for your pupils) and reflective practice (again, for both you and the pupils) in order to understand more deeply the impact the curriculum is having on your teaching and their learning.

2 Establish the wider context of your evaluation and share your evaluation's design

Start any evaluation by trying to define the wider context of your proposed curriculum development. This could involve a number of different activities. First of all, have similar pieces of curriculum development been undertaken elsewhere? If you have not got the time to do significant searching of written or electronic sources, posting a short question on a teacher website/forum (such as the *Times Educational Supplement*) may be worthwhile. Local authority advisers can often have a helpful overview of work that is going on in different schools. Universities with education departments may also be a helpful point of contact. Having read this book is a great start to this process! We have written about key projects drawn from the work of a range of partners throughout the previous chapters. It might be that you could follow up on a few of their stories and research in more detail to help inform your thinking at this early stage.

This leads on to the second key point. Sharing your curriculum unit and the accompanying evaluation framework at an early stage is important. Who might you share this with? In the context of a piece of school-based curriculum development, we would urge you to share you ideas with the senior manager within your school who has a responsibility for the curriculum at the appropriate key stage. While this might have an effect on the political dimension of your work (i.e. you probably do not want to upset your senior managers!), as you are working within a management system where accountability is important they probably have a right to know what is going on. But, more important than that, by sharing your ideas and design at this early stage you are showing yourself to be a reflective teacher, someone who is serious about wanting to initiate change in their teaching in a systematic and responsible way. You may also want to share your thinking about the proposed piece of curriculum development in other forums too. It is helpful to get feedback from a group of colleagues whose judgements you trust and with whom you can share ideas without fear of ridicule or rejection. For secondary school colleagues working in small, or even one-person, departments, sharing your work with teachers who teach your own subject in another school may be another useful source of feedback too.

3 Set out the aims, outcomes and activities of the evaluation

You will be used to setting aims and objectives for your curriculum. Lesson plans have learning objectives; units of work have broader learning objectives; both have learning outcomes. All teaching involves the design of creative and engaging teaching activities through which pupils can learn the key objectives you have set. They will almost certainly learn other things along the way that you have not anticipated!

The skills that you have developed in all of these contexts can be applied to the design of a piece of educational evaluation. You will need to ask yourself general and specific questions about the purpose of the evaluation and what you hope it will achieve. We would strongly recommend that these relate in some way to the broader teaching and learning objectives that you have set for the curriculum unit. It is hard for us to pre-empt what these questions might be without knowing more about your local context and your work, but here are a few suggestions to get you started. You might include general questions such as:

- How has adopting an area-based curriculum approach to this unit impacted on my pupils' learning?
- To what extent has adopting an area-based curriculum facilitated a broader array of educational opportunities for my pupils in this unit?

as well as specific questions such as:

- Precisely what have my pupils been able to achieve in this area-based curriculum unit that they would not have been able to achieve had I run a more traditional unit?
- Is the amount of time and effort that I have put into this area-based curriculum unit worth it in terms of the advantages/disadvantages that it has presented?

Building links between the activities of the curriculum unit and the accompanying evaluation is also a good idea. Typical activities within the unit itself will include various pedagogical elements that you have bought together to promote the learning that you want pupils to engage with. Use these activities to assist in the process of the educational evaluation; in other words, position the activities of the evaluation, whatever they might be (and we will give you three options to consider below), within the teaching activities in an integrated way. Ensuring that the evaluation is embedded within the curriculum unit, rather than being bolted on to the end of it, is the best way. Again, think about this in relation to assessment. Assessment is always better when it is an integral part of the teaching and learning process (as in the assessment for learning strategies that have become common in recent years) rather than being conceptualised and delivered as a separate activity within the classroom.

4 Manage the resources within your evaluation

Thinking about the resources of your evaluation will require you to consider a range of issues. First, and perhaps most importantly, decide on the amount of time that you have to devote to the evaluation of the curriculum unit. Doubtless there will be a whole range of other things that you have to do during the course of an average teaching day and you must ensure that everything is manageable. While you may feel that you have limited time, it is worthwhile to try to allow for a regular period of time during the evaluation for reflection and note-taking. This is better than spending a lot of time at the beginning and end of the project, with nothing or very little in between. Try, when possible, to spread your evaluative time across the whole period.

Although an evaluation of a curriculum unit of this type could be done as an individual venture, perhaps the benefit of collaboration is most keenly felt here. Working with a colleague on a piece of curriculum development has many advantages, not least in sharing the work-load and having that sense of a shared journey along a new educational landscape.

In addition to time, there will be other resources that you can use to assist your evaluation. We would strongly recommend the use of portable audio and video technologies to help you capture key moments within the unit. Much of this could be facilitated with simple software on a computer or a mobile device. Again, involve your pupils in this. Getting them to reflect on their work in progress via reviewing a video of themselves working can be a fascinating experience for student and teacher alike. We will return to this in greater detail below.

Similarly, build in key questions that relate to your evaluation in written feedback that your pupils could provide through their exercise books or folders. Anything that helps you capture an essence or flavour of their work in the unit will help you form a more detailed understanding at a later date. This moves us directly on to our next point: data collection.

5 Collect a range of data about your curriculum unit

Collecting data sounds very grand. In practice, it can be quite simple. Aim to collect data related to the evaluation of your curriculum unit on a regular basis. Remember that evaluative data, like assessment data, can take many shapes and forms. You may have chosen a particular class, or a group of pupils within a class, to be the specific focus for the evaluation of the unit. Whatever you do, keep it manageable and within the allocation of time that you have decided to devote to the evaluation. You might consider keeping a teaching journal for the duration of the evaluation. This could contain short comments about teaching sessions, notes about your thoughts or feelings during the evaluation process, snapshots of conversations with pupils or other things that come to your mind and might be useful later on. This kind of reflective writing can be an invaluable aspect of your evaluation. You will find many other published resources to assist with this aspect of evaluation (e.g. McIntosh 2010; McNiff 2005; Phillips and Carr 2010).

What do you do when you are evaluating your area-based curriculum unit?

Your piece of area-based curriculum development has been set up. You have identified your aims and objectives, chosen your curriculum activities, selected the classes that you are going to work with, got a time-scale to work within and established your available resources. You have shared your ideas with your senior manager and other selected colleagues and reflected on their advice. You are ready to go. So, what are you going to actually do during the evaluation itself? What are the activities that you can undertake, alongside your teaching, to help collect the data that you need to understand more fully the impact of area-based curriculum development?

In this part of the chapter we are going to explore three key activities that you can undertake that are complementary to your teaching role. This complementarity is crucial. Finding the links between teaching and evaluation will help you manage your time effectively and avoid you being distracted from your key role as a teacher in your classroom. It will also make for a better evaluation and assist you in your own development as a teacher. The three activities are:

- Observation
- Communication
- Interviewing

1 Observing your classroom

As teachers, we are used to observing classrooms. It is a key aspect of our work. Effective teachers make time during their lessons to take that step backwards from their teaching role, and from the complexity of the classroom interactions that are occurring between themselves and their pupils, to observe what is going on. Using observation as a key component of your evaluation will greatly enhance your generic teaching abilities.

There is a flip side to this. Familiarity with the classroom can be a barrier to effective observation. Therefore, it will be important to find ways to challenge your own observations, particularly if you are conducting this evaluative work within your own teaching. To this end, we will briefly consider a range of issues associated with observation that will help you to do this.

First, learn to live with uncertainty in your observations. It is quite right and understandable that, on occasions, you will not be able to make sense immediately of what is going on. As we explored above, the notion of 'truth' within an evaluation is highly contestable. What you are watching is framed by notions of objectivity and subjectivity which you could spend a lifetime exploring. You do not have time to do that now! Rather, look for examples of activities which are 'credible and defensible rather than true' (Kushner 1992a, p. 1). Subtleties in your observations can be explored at a later date through the second and third activities discussed below. While you are observing, use your instincts as a teacher to look out for interesting responses that your pupils make within the lesson, unusual responses within particular activities, or that spark of creativity that a student may show at a given moment. Accounting for these in a simple way through your observation notes will be important, even if it is a brief comment in your teaching journal that can be returned to at a later date.

Second, use a range of technology to help you with your observations. As we mentioned above, this could include audio or video recording. The review and analysis of these materials can also reveal interesting material that you may miss in the hurly-burly of a lesson. While this can be a timesaver and assist you to conduct the dual roles of teacher and evaluator, beware of relying too much on this. It takes a long time to review recorded materials and you may not have much time available given your other commitments. But the benefits can be significant if you have the time. Recording yourself as a teacher is no different from those disciplines such as acting, dancing or athletics where video analysis is central to improving performance. Why should it be any different for teachers?

Finally, be focused in your observations. Your area-based curriculum unit has specific aims and objectives. Try and focus on these in the early stages of your observation. But, as we discussed above, remember that these aims and objectives should not be thought of as being fixed in stone. They will develop as the piece of curriculum development unfolds and you will need to be responsive to the outworking of these throughout the curriculum activities that you have designed.

2 Communicate effectively

Like observation, communication is a vital component of effective teaching and learning. Communication can take many forms and you will need to be alert for these throughout your evaluation. Non-verbal forms of communication such as gesture, body language or facial expression will all be evident within your classroom. But verbal communication will probably be a major focus in all evaluations. In particular, conversations between teachers and pupils are an essential part of every classroom context. As such, they present a vital opportunity for evaluation. How can we use the opportunities to converse with pupils to help the process of your evaluation?

First, be as natural as you can be in your conversations with pupils. Clearly, you are still their teacher and this will frame your conversations at a certain level. But build on your existing relationship with the class, or the individual student, and seek to nurture conversations around your key evaluation aims and objectives. Try to do this in a natural, not a forced, way. Do your pupils need to know that you are evaluating a particular approach to curriculum design within these lessons? There will be differences of opinion on this point, but if you feel that this is going to close down their responses (i.e. you think they are going to say what they think you want to hear) then we would suggest not.

Second, take nothing for granted. Listen to the conversations that pupils are having between themselves during the various activities that you have designed within the curriculum unit. Make it your practice not to interrupt them too soon. These conversations often contain really important evidence that can usefully inform your evaluation. When you do intervene, maintain a critical stance and do not close down the possibilities for them to express alternative viewpoints.

Third, do not over-depend on the pupils' voices and forget your own. Recent educational initiatives have given a priority to 'pupil voice' that many educationalists are now finding unhelpful. For some, the emphasis on pupil voice is nothing more than adults' 'copping out' and an 'abdication of their responsibilities' (Paton 2009). While we cannot completely agree with this perspective, it is important to remember that your viewpoint and opinion does matter! So, do not underplay what you think about your own and your pupils' work in your evaluation.

3 Interview pupils

The final key activity for your evaluation ought to be interviewing. Interviewing has a long history in educational research and it can prove to be a very beneficial approach within evaluations too. There are many guides to how to conduct interviews with young people either within educational research (Kvale 2007) or as part of a clinical setting (Ginsburg 1997). There are a number of important points to consider here.

First, interviews that are mainly about information retrieval make a number of assumptions. They assume that the interviewee (in our case, the student) knows something that the interviewer (that's you!) does not know. The task of the interview is to extract that information. Your role might be to put that particular student or pupils at ease, asking them appropriate questions and facilitating the resulting conversation in a way that exposes the information that is deemed important. This is a perfectly legitimate approach to interviewing and one that, given the potential resource constraints that you may find yourself facing, may be the best use of your time.

However, there is a second way that interviews can be conducted that may be even more beneficial. The 'developmental interview' is underpinned by a range of different assumptions. As Kushner explains:

> This approach assumes that interviewee probably does not know either and the task of the interviewer is to set up a learning situation. The interviewee is seen as someone locked up in a role and unable to take an objective role of what he or she knows, so the task of the interview is to prise the person out of the role and to ask them to look back at it and evaluate it. The interview is typified by exploration, by asking many supplementary questions to clarify and extend an idea. ... The focus is on the individual rather than the project – their life and values. The idea is to see the project in the context of the person's life.
>
> (Kushner 1992c, p. 1)

This approach to interviewing is more time-consuming. But, as Kushner points out in a later point in his exposition, it can be conducted over a longer period of time, perhaps as an interview that takes place on a number of separate occasions or stages. For teachers, this type of dialogue with a student could become part of the design of a one-off evaluation of the type we have discussed throughout this chapter. By being asked the right sort of questions, pupils could engage with this type of focus through written responses as well as in a face-to-face interview situation. This may also be less threatening from their perspective and certainly less time-consuming from your point of view.

This moves us on to a final point about interviewing. If you are going to include interviews in your evaluation (and we would encourage you to), try and give them a sense of occasion from the pupils' perspective. In our own evaluation work as a teacher, we would often try and find opportunities outside the formal time of a lesson to talk to pupils about their work. This might include a lunchtime 'interview', where pupils can relax and eat their lunches and you can talk about their work on a particular project. We found that this was more relaxing for us too. Group interviews or focus groups are often better in this respect. Pupils can bounce their ideas off each other and, when this is going well, you can often find yourself taking a back seat in the interview process. This is a good sign that the interview is moving beyond the 'information-retrieval' approach and really entering a developmental phase.

Drawing conclusions from your evaluation

You have reached the end of the evaluation period. You have observed pupils working through the area-based curriculum activities you have planned and delivered, you have talked to them about their work, conducted group interviews with a selected number of pupils, and completed a teaching journal throughout the evaluation. In a parallel stream of activity perhaps, you have being assessing your pupils' work in formative and summative ways. Your assessment data is collated and organised and you have been able to provide the appropriate top-level data to your senior manager. You are faced with a collection of data drawn from your assessment and evaluative processes. It is time to make some judgements about your process of area-based curriculum development.

One of the key ways of making judgements in this situation is to ask yourself questions about the data you have collected. Perhaps this is easier when you are working collaboratively, but it certainly possible to do this individually too. In relation to your piece of area-based curriculum development, the following types of questions may be useful to consider at this moment:

- Was this the appropriate time for a piece of curriculum development for me (as a teacher), for my pupils, my department and my school? How can I be sure?
- What are the consequences of the changes I have made for myself, my pupils and my colleagues?
- How do the changes that I have advocated relate to other changes that we are being asked to make?
- Where do the values come from that underpin this piece of curriculum development? Are they from my experiences or beliefs, or are they from somewhere else? If so, can I pinpoint precisely where they have originated from?
- Who have been the winners and losers in this piece of curriculum development?
- How has the teaching and learning been connected in this piece of curriculum development? How do I know?
- How would I describe the teaching approach I have adopted throughout this curriculum unit? Has it been authoritarian or democratic, formal or informal? What aspects of my pedagogy have changed or developed from my traditional, subject-based pedagogy?
- How have my pupils learnt in this project? In what ways have they learnt differently from those that might have been in evidence in a more traditional approach to the same topic? What have I learnt from the whole experience?

- Were my original aims, objectives and activities for the curriculum unit appropriate? Did they change or develop over the duration of the unit?
- Whose knowledge really counts within a piece of curriculum development like this? How did the knowledge base of my own subject(s) or phase relate to the area-based curriculum unit I had planned?
- If this was a piece of curriculum development that I did on my own, would it have worked better as a piece of collaborative curriculum development? If it was collaborative in its structure, can I conceive of it working more effectively as an independent activity? Could the collaborative dimensions of the project be translated into an individual teacher's pedagogical approach?

These questions may or may not be appropriate for the piece of curriculum development that you have undertaken. Learning to ask the right questions about the work you have undertaking is part of the process of reaching a judgement about the project. It may be that you could adapt some of the above questions for your own work. You may need to invent your own.

This questioning process can continue for some time. Pragmatically, you are going to have to draw a line under this at some point and move forwards. But reaching a conclusion, in your mind or as a written report of the evaluation, is an important final step. I would encourage you to write up the evaluation, however briefly, as an integral part of this process. For Stenhouse, educational research was 'systematic enquiry made public' (Stenhouse 1983). The 'making public' part of this definition is crucial, partly because it provides a system of accountability but, more importantly, because making your findings public will help create a dialogue of ideas about teaching and learning that will benefit yourself and others.

So, as a final part of this evaluative process, submit a short report to your senior managers but also look out for opportunities to share your work with other teachers. At a recent meeting of the governing body on which one of us serves, we received an article, via the head teacher's termly report, from a mathematics teacher working at the school. Her evaluative study had looked at the process of implementing a more explicit assessment for learning approach within her teaching of mathematics. The report was a scholarly account of her approach, characterised by many of the attributes that we have discussed throughout this chapter. The student voice was very evident within her study, but also her own, professional opinions shone through, backed up with evidence drawn from various sources of data. Having completed the study, this teacher was asked to present her work and associated findings to the rest of the staff within the school. Her approach was adopted and adapted to help provide a broader assessment for learning strategy within the school as a whole. Through various external links that the school had, she was invited to attend a meeting of local authority advisory staff and present her work to them. This was well received and further studies are being planned.

This type of approach empowers the individual teacher. In a political era of top-down educational initiatives, it reasserts the authority of the teacher and places them at the centre of the process of curriculum development. It does take time but it is time richly rewarded for you and your pupils.

Conclusion

Congratulations on reaching the end of our book on area-based approaches to curriculum development. We hope you have enjoyed it and found it useful.

Area-based approaches to curriculum development are, in one sense, a new form of curriculum development that presents exciting opportunities for schools. But, as we have shown, these approaches relate closely to key principles of curriculum development. If Stenhouse was right, and there really is no curriculum development without teacher development, then the converse is true too. There is no teacher development without curriculum development. Most teachers we meet want to inspire their pupils and encourage them to learn to their full potential. Equally, they want to enjoy a long and sustained teaching career. One of the keys for having that type of career is to avoid stagnating.

Done in the right way, curriculum development can be a powerful motivating force in your development as a teacher. Linking curriculum development to key themes drawn from your school and your pupils' local area is a way of grounding the curriculum in their lived experience both within and beyond school. It is a way of mitigating the negative effects of that inside/outside school boundary that is often so keenly felt by pupils. Throughout this book, we have exemplified a range of approaches that you might want to start with as you explore this approach. In this final chapter we have given you a set of basic evaluation tools to monitor your progress. We would be delighted to hear about your own curriculum development activities in these areas, so please contact us with your stories. Until then, enjoy your teaching!

References

Ginsburg, H. P. (1997) *Entering the Child's Mind: The clinical interview in psychological research and practice*. Cambridge, Cambridge University Press.

Kushner, S. (1992a) 'Section 5: Making observations'. *The Arts, Education and Evaluation: An introductory pack with practical exercises*. Norwich, Centre for Applied Research in Education, University of East Anglia.

Kushner, S. (1992b) 'Section 6: Interviewing'. *The Arts, Education and Evaluation: An introductory pack with practical exercises*. Norwich, Centre for Applied Research in Education, University of East Anglia.

Kvale, S. (2007) *Doing Interviews*. London, Sage.

McIntosh, P. (2010) *Action Research and Reflective Practice*. London, Routledge.

McNiff, J. (2005) *Action Research for Teachers*. London, Routledge.

Paton, G. (2009) 'Adults "Abdicating Responsibility" for Children'. www.telegraph.co.uk/education/6598138/Adults-abdicating-responsibility-for-children.html [last accessed 10 December 2009].

Phillips, D. K. and Carr, K. (2010) *Becoming a Teacher through Action Research*. London, Routledge.

Stenhouse, L. (1975) *An Introduction to Curriculum Research and Development*. London, Heinemann Educational.

Stenhouse, L. (1983) 'Research is Systematic Enquiry Made Public'. *British Educational Research Journal* 9:1, pp. 11–20.

Stenhouse, L. (1985) *Research as a Basis for Teaching*. London, Heinemann Educational Books.

Index

Page numbers in *italics* denote tables.

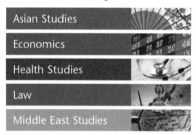